"*Pure in Heart* is honest, hopeful, and helpful. Kell is joyfully and carefully God-centered and direct. He does not give the false hope of simple, immediate answers. In fact, this thoughtful book will challenge you with its questions. It carefully exposes distortions and reminds us of practices that can help—the role of the local congregation, confession to God, and confession to others. Kell reminds us of the freedom from sin we already know, and shows us how it is worth the cost of any repentance. Read this; it's worth your time."

Mark Dever, Pastor, Capitol Hill Baptist Church; President, 9Marks Ministries

"If you're looking for a resource on sexual purity written by someone who's never struggled, this is not the book for you. Garrett Kell has been in the trenches. And while he's enjoyed a great measure of deliverance, the smoke of battle still lingers over his life. *Pure in Heart* directs our gaze to the promise, spoken and secured by Jesus, that the pure in heart will see God. Laced with vivid illustrations and saturated with Scripture, Garrett brings years of pastoral wisdom to a topic we often wish to avoid. If you're looking for a resource that will reinvigorate your heart with biblical truth and concrete steps for the fight, this is the book for you."

Matt Smethurst, Managing Editor, The Gospel Coalition; Pastor, River City Baptist Church, Richmond, Virginia; author, *Deacons* and *Before You Open Your Bible*

"This is a book we were hoping Kell would write and one that we're praying every member of our church will read. The content is not mere theory—Garrett Kell has struggled himself, and helps others fight for purity. *Pure in Heart* redirects our eyes off this world and onto Christ as the only one who can satisfy our souls. In a world where we're bombarded with impure images, this book is an excellent reminder that when we fight for purity, we see God. Whether you struggle in this area or not, read this book, and then pass it on to a friend."

Dave and Gloria Furman, Senior Pastor, Redeemer Church of Dubai; author, *Being There* and *Kiss the Wave*; and his wife, Gloria, author, *Alive in Him*

T0367151

"From the pulpit to the pew, sexual sin is a gaping wound within the lives of countless men and women. Seemingly insignificant at the beginning, it grows into a gangrene of darkness that seems incurable. *Pure in Heart* is like a surgeon's scalpel flaying open the wound of sin, administering the promises of God, and applying the balm of the gospel of Christ. Revealing his own venerable wounds, Garrett Kell uses biblical and theologically precise truth for those hurting from the past, battling in the present, and desiring freedom in the future. His message is simple: there is hope and healing in Christ."

Dustin Benge, Provost, Union School of Theology, Wales

"Garrett Kell comes alongside you in this book as a kind, thoughtful, and wise older brother who's not immune to struggles with sexual purity himself. This is Bible-infused, gospel-centered gold—helpful, practical, and encouraging writing that raises the bar, saturates with grace, and shines the spotlight on Jesus."

Shelby Abbott, campus minister; author, *Pressure Points* and *DoubtLess*

"*Pure in Heart* faithfully opens the Scriptures to expose the sin that hinders us from seeing God. Yet rather than leave us to despair, Kell points to Jesus, who is able to make us pure. Marked by urgency and practical wisdom, this book encourages the church to see that Jesus is enough as she fights for purity."

Harshit Singh, Pastor, Satyan Vachan Church, Lucknow, India

"We unreservedly recommend Garrett Kell's book to anyone struggling with sexual purity. We do so because it is an honest and transparent book written by someone who has struggled in this area and achieved genuine victory. This victory was not through a self-help program but through the gospel of our Lord Jesus Christ. What we also love about this book is that it pleads with those wrestling with sexual impurity to come out of hiding and seek the help of God's people. It is in the loving community of the church that the wounded are healed."

Conrad and Felistas Mbewe, Pastor, Kabwata Baptist Church, Lusaka, Zambia; and his wife, Felistas

"*Pure in Heart* is clear, honest, and direct, revealing both the severity of sexual sin as well as the beauty of God's grace. This biblically rooted guide, practical at its core, delightfully guides anyone who reads it into an encouraging route to freedom from sexual bondage. Garrett Kell shows the reader a roadmap to truth and grace; his book is a great gift to share with anyone who seeks gospel truth in the relationship between God, mankind, sin, grace, and sexuality."

Christopher Yuan, speaker; author, *Holy Sexuality and the Gospel: Sex, Desire, and Relationships Shaped by God's Grand Story*

"I know from my pastoral and discipleship ministry to young people—and from personal experience—just how devastating pornography and other sexual sin can be. This is why I'm incredibly grateful to God for Garrett Kell's new book, *Pure in Heart*. It brings biblical wisdom, pastoral insights, and practical applications to bear in the battle every believer must fight against the lusts that distract us from the glory of the Savior who loves us."

Jared C. Wilson, Director, Pastoral Training Center, Liberty Baptist Church, Kansas City, Missouri; author, *The Imperfect Disciple*

"This is an honest, practical, and challenging book that continuously points the reader to Christ. Drawing from his own experiences, Garrett has produced something that is easy to read and extremely relevant. We both highly recommend this book."

Mez and Miriam McConnell, Niddrie Community Church, Scotland, United Kingdom

"This book is thoroughly biblical, refreshingly personal, full of grace and truth, and focused on what matters most: seeing God and experiencing full happiness in him. Toward that ultimate end, we both gladly commend this book to you, men and women alike."

David and Heather Platt, Pastor, McLean Bible Church; author, *Radical*; and his wife, Heather

"Once we allow sin to come into our lives as a supplicant, it will remain as a tyrant. The Bible has taught this since the very beginning. However, it also teaches that, with the grace of Christ, sin can be overcome. Garrett Kell's book is not only for those who have already fallen into temptation, but it's also for those who are being tempted. Biblical, honest, straight to the point, this book needs to be read by all who love the Lord and struggle against impurity of the heart."

Jonas Madureira, Professor of Philosophy, Mackenzie Presbyterian University; Senior Pastor, Word Baptist Church, São Paulo, Brazil

Pure in Heart

Sexual Sin and the Promises of God

J. Garrett Kell

WHEATON, ILLINOIS

Library of Congress Cataloging-in-Publication Data

Names: Kell, J. Garrett, author.
Title: Pure in heart : sexual sin and the promises of God / J. Garrett Kell.
Description: Wheaton, Illinois : Crossway, 2021. | Includes bibliographical references and index.
Identifiers: LCCN 2020043972 (print) | LCCN 2020043973 (ebook) | ISBN 9781433574894 (trade paperback) |
    ISBN 9781433574900 (pdf) | ISBN 9781433574917 (mobipocket) | ISBN 9781433574924 (epub)
Subjects: LCSH: Sex—Biblical teaching. | Sex—Religious aspects—Christianity. | Sexual ethics. | Sin—Christianity. |
    Spiritual life—Christianity.
Classification: LCC BS2545.S36 K45 2021 (print) | LCC BS2545.S36 (ebook) | DDC 241/.66—dc23
LC record available at https://lccn.loc.gov/2020043972
LC ebook record available at https://lccn.loc.gov/2020043973

| VP | | 30 | 29 | 28 | 27 | 26 | 25 | 24 | 23 | 22 | 21 |
| 15 | 14 | 13 | 12 | 11 | 10 | 9 | 8 | 7 | 6 | 5 | 4 | 3 | 2 |

For Christ's bride, the church.
May we present ourselves pure to him.

Contents

Acknowledgments

AS A SEASHORE IS SHAPED by the endless influence of breaking waves, so I have been shaped by many influences. Supremely, my heavenly Father rescued me from my sinful wandering through the grace of his Son and the power of his Spirit. Since that day, his kind providences have guided my every step.

Next to my Savior, no one has affected me more than my beloved wife, Carrie. She knows the best of me, and the worst, yet she loves me still. Her wisdom has marked me, and her continual forgiveness serves as a living reminder of God's love for me in Christ.

My children are still young, yet regularly show me God's love. I pray they will avoid the snares I have endured and that Jesus will be their refuge, as he has been mine. Eden, Haddon, Phoebe, Graham, and Simeon—walk with Jesus; he will never lead you astray.

My father, mother, and sister comprise a wonderful family in which hospitality, tough love, hard work, and lots of laughs were commonplace. I remember our days with joy.

In his church, God has given me family, friends, and mentors. Tom Nelson took me in as a spiritual son after my conversion. He taught me nearly every book of the Bible and instilled in me a love and trust in God's word that I cannot imagine living without.

In my darkest hour, God introduced me to John Henderson. John showed me from the Scriptures how the gospel applies to a believer's brokenness. I am eternally grateful to you.

Seven years into my ministry, Mark Dever befriended me and opened his life and ministry to my family. Mark has modeled for me what it means to be a pastor. He has shown me how to love God's flock with truth, courage, tenderness, and intentional care.

The congregations of Denton Bible, Graham Bible, Capitol Hill Baptist, and Del Ray Baptist have loved me and built me up in Christ. I praise God for those churches.

In each church, God has privileged me to labor alongside godly elders who provided friendship, accountability, encouragement, and needed rebuke. Chris Disch, Ben Hamilton, Jason Seville, Mercury Payton, Eric Butterbaugh, Joshua Chatman, Shai Linne, David Verhey, Reagan Kelley, Dean Hufstedler, Tommy Grace, Will Lunsford, Zach Schlegel, Warren Nystrom, and many others have uniquely served my soul.

Outside those churches are friends without whom I cannot fathom being the man I am today. Among them are David Light, Shelby Abbott, Kerry Lee Lewis, Reid Monaghan, Brian Davis, Matthew Martens, and a nursing-home widow named Mama Ruth.

Finally, editors are a writer's best friend. Matt Smethurst, Ben Robin, Heather Robinson, Steve Coleman, and Johnny Antle have worked to make my feeble efforts more faithful.

To those mentioned, and many more, I am greatly indebted. To God be all glory.

Introduction

EARLY IN HOMER'S *ODYSSEY*, Ulysses receives a warning of dangers awaiting him on the journey to Ithaca. A certain island must be avoided at all costs. It's an enchanting place inhabited by Sirens—dangerous creatures who sing a beautiful song to passing sailors.

Their song, however, is a trap. It captivates the hearers and lures them closer. Once at the feet of the Sirens, the victims are shackled, not by chains but by their desire to hear more of the melody. The intoxicating music overtakes the sailors' senses, leaving them to die beside the victims of ages past.

As Ulysses nears the forbidden island, his curiosity eclipses the warning. He orders the crew to plug their ears with wax before fastening him to the mast, so he can hear the Sirens sing. When the island finally comes into view and he hears the Sirens' song, his sobriety fades and he becomes hypnotized by their call to draw closer.

Though Ulysses can see the pile of bones at the Sirens' feet, he longs to move closer. He fights against the restraints. More of the enticing song is all he wants. Yet mercifully, the restraints hold long enough for his ship to sail past and for Ulysses to regain his senses.

The themes of this mythical tale may sound familiar to you. Like the song of the Sirens, the temptation to sexual sin cries out, summoning listeners to come and take their fill of fleeting, deadly pleasures. It tickles the ears of men and women, young and old, godly and godless. At times the seductive song of sexual lust seems irresistible. What are we to do? White-knuckled willpower cannot restrain our desires.

My Ear for the Song

Sadly, I know the song of the Sirens all too well. My first exposure to pornography was at age nine. I still remember the sunlight glaring on the wrinkled magazine a friend had stolen from his father.

Corrupted curiosity awoke in me that day. The next twelve years were devoted to feeding my lustful hunger. Yet no picture or fantasy or relationship could fulfill me; in fact, my longing only grew. At times I controlled my lusts, but more often I imitated the blind men clawing at Lot's door, scrambling to satisfy their passions (Gen. 19:11). I indulged every desire I could and used anyone I needed to in the process. I was a liar, a cheat, and a perverted manipulator.

Thankfully, the God of grace intervened in my life through the witness of a friend, and I met the Savior who shed his blood for Siren-lovers like me. I began to walk with Jesus and love him. He transformed my life and introduced me to the sweetness of his holiness. I quickly learned, however, that old loves die slowly. I delighted in hearing the voice of the Shepherd, but—to my shame—my ear remained tuned to the song of the Siren.

One Wednesday morning still scars my memory. I was a three-year-old Christian and had just begun seminary. I attended an early morning Bible study, but no later than the final Amen did the Siren's song reach my ears. At this time in my life, though, the song had changed key. It used to come as an invitation; now it came as a command. I felt as if I had no choice but to obey its orders.

I went home from Bible study that morning and looked at pornography for hours—page after empty page, feasting on the mirage of sin. Afterward I was left with a horrifying thought: *I guess I'll always be like this.* Sin had sapped all hope that freedom in Christ was actually possible.

But I wanted freedom—so I employed every tactic I could. I tried cold showers. I increased exercise. I joined a legalistic club (we put a dollar in the "pervert pot" if we compromised). I listened to purity pep talks and searched for magical Bible verses—but all to no real avail. To my shame, some of my most grievous sins were committed against the Savior *after* he made me his own. I needed something more powerful than man-powered tactics to help me.

A Sweeter Song

In 2007, the Lord graciously intervened. I was three years into pastoring a church in a small Texas town. Though the ministry was thriving, I was hiding my dark secret. Sure, I confessed to friends that I was "struggling with purity," but I assured them the worst of it was "in the past."

In truth, however, I was deceived. My pride and fear of man kept me from being honest about how deep my darkness had become. I assumed that because I loved Jesus—I was a *pastor*, after all—I would be able to overcome it. But I couldn't. Eventually, God led me to confide my entire struggle to a pastor friend in another city, then used him to help me be honest with my own elders, which eventually resulted in confessing my sin before the whole church I was pastoring.

What followed was probably the worst year of my life. My reputation became ruined. Worst of all, I saw how my sin had shattered some of my closest friends' trust in Jesus. The refining furnace of God's mercy burned brightly in me, and after the brutal year had passed, I was left with a peaceful fruit of righteousness that could have come no other way (Heb. 12:10–11). I knew I'd been forgiven through Christ's blood, but until then I didn't understand that the good news is just as much for *believers* as it is for unbelievers. Through the brokenness, I began to hear the song of grace as a better, sweeter tune than the song of sin.

What followed was a small revival, surely in my heart, but also in our church. In several ways God emptied us of hypocrisy and led many to repent of their own sins. It is true that "where sin increase[s], grace abounds all the more" (Rom. 5:20).[1]

I share all of this because I hope you will see that this book is not birthed out of a squeaky-clean study, much less an impeccable ivory tower. It comes from the wrestlings of a wanderer. It comes from someone God has graciously helped.

The Lord has brought other brothers and sisters alongside me and lifted my eyes to see that he provides a pathway to a better beauty than lust. And that pathway is found in this promise: "Blessed are the pure in heart, for they shall see God" (Matt. 5:8).

Seeing God by Pursuing Purity

As you hold this book, Jesus's promise is for you. Whether you're reading to help someone else or to find hope for yourself, God de-

---

1   To read more about this story, see my article "I Was a Pastor Hooked on Porn," The Gospel Coalition website, August 22, 2017, www.thegospelcoalition.org/article/i-was-pastor-hooked-on-porn/.

lights in helping you. He desires us to see him more clearly, which is why he gives us this precious promise. He wants us to know how to enjoy sex, avoid sin, and love him. Jesus's promise in Matthew 5:8 provides wisdom for the pursuit.

This book is arranged in two sections, each meditating on his promise. The first section points us to the *promise of purity*. This lays the foundation for understanding who God is, what he promises, and what makes pursuing sexual purity so difficult. While you may be tempted to skim this section, I encourage you not to jump ahead to the "practical" suggestions in the second section. As with building a sturdy home, a solid foundation is essential.

The second section introduces long-term strategies for pursuing purity and resisting temptation. I call them *pathways to purity*, since completing a checklist or flipping a switch doesn't accomplish change. Rather, we need radical approaches to killing sin and delighting in the beauty of God. These strategies—applied by faith over time, in the context of a healthy church community—will prove to do what wax earplugs and the restraining ropes of self-effort cannot. God will use these concrete steps to transform your heart, and your life.

Finally, throughout this book you'll find real-life examples of men and women, single and married, straight and those struggling with same-sex attraction. You may not relate to all of them, but my prayer is that God will use something here to help you see him more clearly—and to help others do the same. Holiness is a community project, and fostering an informed empathy is a vital part of loving both one another and the King who invites us to behold his beauty.

Let's begin our journey of seeing him.

PART 1

PROMISE OF PURITY

1

Promise

*"I have spread my couch with coverings. . . . I have
perfumed my bed with myrrh, aloes, and cinnamon.
Come, let us take our fill of love till morning."*
THE SEDUCTRESS (PROV. 7:16–18)

"Blessed are the pure in heart, for they shall see God."
JESUS (MATT. 5:8)

COMPETING VOICES CALL TO US. They offer promises. One is
calling from heaven, the other from hell. We must choose which
voice to follow.

Sarah felt trapped in her marriage. Passion for her husband grew
cold while passion for a coworker warmed. Each day the coworker
complimented her. He noticed her appearance and sought her company.
The attention awakened something in her she thought long dead.
Sarah liked it. She wanted more of it, though she knew it was wrong.

Slowly she walked along a perilous precipice of temptation. On the one side: intrigue and seduction. On the other: the voice of the good shepherd, summoning her to the sweetness of his pastures.

Truly Blessed

A temptation invites us to sin against God while promising happiness apart from God. The lips of the seductress "drip honey, / and her speech is smoother than oil" (Prov. 5:3). She knows exactly what to say—and how to say it. Slyly she affirms our attractiveness and importance. Escaping with her holds endless possibilities for enjoyment. You can bend the rules; she promises not to tell. Restrain sexual passion? That would be unnatural and unnecessary, she insists. The offer of her embrace is an invitation to ecstasy.

Now, Jesus also fulfills our passions and serves our pleasures, but of a distinctly different kind and in a vastly different way. "Blessed are the pure in heart," he proclaims. The happiness he offers is unique. It cannot be known apart from holiness, and it arises from faith and obedience. It requires devotion, a willingness to forsake the flash of instant fulfillment for a joy that cannot be seen or tasted or touched.

The word *blessed* is rich with meaning. It refers to a deep and happy fulfillment. This kind of happiness does not blow away with the wind; it weathers the storms of life. It looks to riches stored in heaven, not on earth. The blessed person of Matthew 5 looks to God for satisfaction.

Why are the pure in heart blessed? Because "they shall see God." According to Jesus, God will bless those who pursue clearer sight of his glory. In other words, the sinful images we seek or forbidden embraces we crave are illusory. They do not provide true blessedness—especially that of seeing God.

Jesus invites us to "taste and see that the LORD is good" (Ps. 34:8). Follow his commands, he beckons, "that [his] joy may be in you, and that your joy may be full" (John 15:11). Embracing his promise requires trust in his promises over and against sin's promises.

Sin draws strength from the promise of immediate satisfaction. It offers a retreat from reality, whispering, *You deserve it.* Lust assures that a rendezvous with secret sin will not be costly, and a return to the Lord will be easy—or unnecessary. *God is love, so he will certainly forgive you, right?* But drinking sin's lies only leaves us longing for more. A glass of saltwater may look promising to a thirsty man, but it only leaves him more parched. Jesus's promises offer us a better drink. His living water does not turn our soul's tongue dry, but refreshes it with everlasting happiness.

The question is simple: *Will you believe his promise?*

Sarah wrestled to believe God's word. She read about the destruction promised to adulterers, but she was certain she could stop at any time. Yet with every deleted text message and inappropriate encounter, her resolve slowly faded. Her flesh screamed for more, and assured her any indulgence would be worth it.

Promise for Then—and Now

Again, sin can offer only immediate satisfaction. Sure, forbidden fruit is exhilarating when you bite into it, but its sweetness quickly vanishes. The bitter aftertaste of pornography or adultery—which seemed so promising at first—now haunts many of us. Sin promises sweetness, but its pleasure expires immediately and its aftertaste is always bitter. This is where we discover a chink in its armor. It has nothing to offer you down the road but regret and shame. As Matt

Smethurst has said, "Sin always looks better through the windshield than the rearview mirror."[1]

God's promises are better. "Blessed are the pure in heart, for they shall see God" is a promise for the present and for the future. One day, the dim mirror of this life will give way to an unveiled encounter with the Lord (1 Cor. 13:12). Our "eyes will behold the king in his beauty" and we shall "see the glory of the LORD, / the majesty of our God" (Isa. 33:17; 35:2). Jesus's promise of blessing for the pure in heart has that coming day in mind. A day when faith becomes sight and hope is fully realized. A day when sin will be a memory and temptation silenced forever. Sin's corruption will be destroyed along with all desire to sin again.

Imagine being enraptured into the Trinitarian love that knows neither beginning nor end. Glory! "He will dwell" among us and will forever "be our God," and forevermore we shall "see his face" (see Rev. 21–22). Those who love God are promised such a day.

But his promise is also for today. Right now, the pure in heart shall see God. Today we can know the blessedness—the happiness—of purity. I didn't always believe this promise. I felt powerless over porn's seduction and was easily charmed by the thrill of the moment. I conceded to being a child of God in chains. But Jesus came to free people like me from Satan's propaganda.

Today, Jesus lays before your heart a more compelling beauty than the seductress. Yes, sin's offering *feels* like it will fulfill you, but God's offering *will*. You will never regret resisting sin. You will

---

1   Matt Smethurst (@MattSmethurst), *Twitter*, December 21, 2017, 9:44 a.m., twitter.com/MattSmethurst/status/943854703540088832.

always regret giving in. I have never looked back on obedience with regret, nor on compromise with gratitude. Seeing God is both our eternal destiny and our daily delight.

God's wisdom merges the promised *then* and present *now* in a way that strengthens us. Consider the words of the apostle John:

> Beloved, *we are God's children now*, and what we will be has *not yet appeared*; but we know that when he appears we shall be like him, because we shall see him as he is. And everyone who thus hopes in him purifies himself as he is pure. (1 John 3:2–3)

Longing to see God on *that day* propels his people to purity *today*. As we long to be with him *then*, we loathe for sin to be with us *now*. Hope in his presence *then* forces us to crucify anything that would make us unlike Jesus *now*. The promise associated with purity gives calendar-spanning hope.

Purity Clarified

Throughout the ages, religious subcultures have both tolerated and perpetuated clouded conceptions of purity. Some churches and "Christian" movements have forbidden sex apart from procreation, encouraged fleeing temptation in monasteries, or even outlawed marriage for church leaders. In the 1990s, thousands of teenage Christians vowed to wear "purity rings" as a pledge of abstinence until marriage. This well-intended gesture presented a narrow understanding of purity. For some, it gave the wrong impression that refusing to "go all the way" before marriage was enough to be pure. Those who embraced this perception of purity could have been prone to either pompous self-righteousness, if they kept on the right side of the line, or profound shame, if they caved to their passion.

But according to the Scriptures, purity can't be reduced to a pledge to keep our pants on. Yes, God calls us to purity in our actions, but he also demands it in our affections. This, I believe, is a fuller understanding:

Purity is an orientation of the faith-filled heart that flees the pleasures of sin and pursues the pleasures of God by the power of the Holy Spirit.

For too long, I assumed "being pure" meant staying within a collection of lines in the sand. If I didn't have extramarital sex or look at hardcore pornography or masturbate, then I was pure and kept God happy. If I crossed one of those lines, though, I dirtied myself and irritated him. This perspective produced a wearisome tossing between self-righteous assurance (when things were going well) and shameful guilt (when they weren't). But Jesus teaches that purity is a posture of the heart, not a line in the sand.

Consider Jesus's teaching on sexual purity: "You have heard that it was said, 'You shall not commit adultery.' But I say to you that everyone who looks at a woman with lustful intent has already committed adultery with her in his heart" (Matt. 5:27–28).

According to Jesus, sexual purity entails far more than virginity until marriage. Never masturbating or watching porn or committing adultery or experimenting with homosexuality are mere tips of the iceberg. Those are godly ambitions, but they're not purity of heart. But Satan tempts us to reduce purity to mere dos and don'ts. He wants us to think lightly of wandering glances and to minimize forays into porn that aren't "hardcore." As long as we don't take off clothes or "go all the way," Satan assures us, we're just fine.

In high school and college, conversations about sex often reveal ignorance of real purity. Hearing the command to "abstain from sexual immorality" (1 Thess. 4:3), students often ask, "Okay, but how far is too far?" In other words, "How close can I get to sin before I'm really in trouble?" Far better, though, are questions like these:

- "What would please God and show my love for him?"
- "Does what I do with my body bring God honor?"
- "Will doing this help me, and others, to better see God?"

In recent years, pondering one particular question has revealed my own heart:

- "If you had one hour to do anything you wanted, and would face no consequences, what would you do?"

I don't know about you, but that question exposes an abiding darkness in me. Too often I resist porn or sexual flings for fear of consequences to my life rather than fear of the Lord. This isn't to say fear of consequences can never be a helpful motivation, but simply abstaining from sin for this reason, or because I don't have access to it, is not the same as being pure in heart.

Sarah's adultery only happened after a thousand small steps toward a mirage of happiness. Her mental boundaries slowly toppled as her heart was taken captive by the thrill of fleeting pleasure. And once ensnared in the darkness, she felt there was no way out.

Purity Is a Pathway
Hear this: purity is not the end—it is a means. Jesus said, "Blessed are the pure in heart, *for* they shall see God." The word "for" tells

us that purity is the *cause*, or *explanation*, for seeing God. The implication is clear: purity is a pathway to seeing God.

Purity for purity's sake is a powerful form of self-serving idolatry that hinders us from seeing God. Jesus continually rebuked religious leaders for being outwardly clean but inwardly dead (see Matt. 23:27–28). We must not succumb to the same trap of settling for mere external purity. Not wanting to confess sin or feel guilt or face consequences has nothing to do with God. It is an empty ambition that stokes pride and weakens your ability to slay sexual temptation.

What we need instead is to fix our eyes on the beauty of God himself. We must kill the sin that tempts us to look away from him—and we kill it *by* looking at him. The battle begins in our hearts and demands diligent effort. Purity will not just happen. We must fight for it.

Satan is laboring to blind you from seeing God today. He raises doubts and whispers promises laced with lies. But we must "resist the devil," and "by the Spirit . . . put to death the deeds of the body," and "strive for . . . the holiness without which no one will see the Lord" (James 4:7; Rom. 8:13; Heb. 12:14). We fight for purity because it leads to seeing God.

Purity requires fleeing both from sin and to God. We "flee from sexual immorality" and "flee youthful passions" (1 Cor. 6:18; 2 Tim. 2:22). But we also unite abstaining from sin with the equally important command to indulge in God. We are not created to simply "not eat" forbidden things, but first and foremost to freely eat all of God's good provisions (see Gen. 2:15–17). Losing this perspective saps motivation for the journey.

So I must ask, Is God your greatest delight? Does your heart long to know and enjoy him? Can you say, with the psalmist, "Because your steadfast love is better than life, / my lips will praise you" (Ps. 63:3)? Do you believe God is better than porn, better than sexual pleasure, better than another human to hold you at night?

If your answer is no, then I encourage you to keep reading. This book is not a magic spell to fix all your struggles, but it contains truth God can use to help you. Keep digging. Keep praying. Keep asking for help.

Augustine said, "You have made us for Yourself, and our hearts are restless until they rest in you."[2] Whether you are a believer in Jesus or not, your heart will find rest only in God himself. Jesus lays before you a promise that will give rest to your weary soul. He died on the cross for all the ways we have traded God for lesser loves, and then he rose to show us the way to enjoy his presence, both now and forevermore.

The hope and power that set Sarah free were contained in the promises of Jesus Christ. As her idol began to betray her, God mercifully reached into her brokenness and gave her eyes of faith to see him. Repentance began when he helped her realize that purity was not a stifling prison, but a pathway to lasting joy.

2 Augustine, *Confessions*, trans. J. G. Pilkington, in vol. 1 of *The Nicene and Post-Nicene Fathers*, Series 1, ed. Philip Schaff (Buffalo, NY: Christian Literature Publishing, 1887), 1.1.1.

2

Sight

"In your light do we see light."
PSALM 36:9

GROWING UP IN WEST VIRGINIA, my boyhood summers were spent exploring the mountains. Rocks, rivers, and trails were our playground. One afternoon a friend and I discovered what we hoped was a cave along a rocky hillside.

With the aid of a flashlight, we pressed into the cold tunnel on our hands and knees. Our excitement grew as the tunnel opened into something resembling an underground cathedral. The cave's ceiling rose high above us while entrances to other tunnels were visible in the distance. It was a dream world for young boys like us.

When the flashlight began to flicker, our dream became a nightmare. The chamber grew dim as we struggled to retrace our steps. The shadows thickened and before we knew it, we were surrounded by a darkness that words cannot capture. Terror made the air seem thick. Our breathing became labored. We were certain the cave would become our tomb.

In what I now know to be God's mercy, a dim sliver of light pierced the darkness long enough for us to locate and stumble toward the small tunnel leading to safety. Once free, we stood in the sun's light, weeping with joy and breathing the fresh air.

See the Light

Being grasped by sin can feel like being trapped in a cave. It takes hold of us in a way that seems overwhelming and inescapable. It hampers our spiritual vision. Indulging sin invites a kind of spiritual darkness that diminishes and sometimes extinguishes the hope, peace, and happiness of God.

Escape from this darkness is only possible when a greater power intervenes. We need supernatural light to shine into our darkness and lead us to freedom. Jesus is the light. "In him was life, and the life was the light of men. The light shines in the darkness, and the darkness has not overcome it" (John 1:4–5).

Seeing God is a promise for the pure in heart—but seeing God is also the means by which our hearts are purified. The way to escape sin's darkness is by beholding the light of the glory of Jesus. It is by seeing his beauty, power, majesty, holiness, and glory that we are transformed. Consider 2 Corinthians 3:18: "We all, with unveiled face, beholding the glory of the Lord, are being transformed into the same image from one degree of glory to another." God removes the veil of unbelief so that his glory shines into our hearts. As 2 Corinthians 4:6 explains, "God, who said, 'Let light shine out of darkness,' has shone in our hearts to give the light of the knowledge of the glory of God in the face of Jesus Christ."

By showing us his glory in the face of Jesus, God transforms us into people who love light rather than darkness. The glory of Jesus captivates our hearts, ruins our taste for sin's promising pleasures, and grows our desire for him more than sin.

Narcissus was a mythical figure famous for his handsome appearance. Admirers celebrated his beauty and longed to be loved by him, but he spurned them all. One day, he came to a stream for a drink and as he knelt, he saw his reflection for the first time. Narcissus's fascination with his own beauty proved to be fatal, as he was never able to pull away from the bank of the reflecting river.

We are all Narcissus with our sin. We become captivated and consumed with our sinful desires, certain they will satisfy despite being ever illusive. For this reason, one taste of pornography is never enough. Sin offers an oasis of pleasure but proves to be a mirage of sorrow. But God calls us to look away from sinful self-indulgence. Instead, we are to look up and behold the life-giving glory of Jesus and be transformed. Second Corinthians 3:18 teaches us several important lessons.

We Become What We Behold

The psalmist warns that when we look to idols, we become like them (Ps. 115:4, 8). Meditating on pornography or sinful fantasies shapes us. Pornography is satanic discipleship. It trains us to see people and situations in perverted ways and become calloused to the way it grieves God. But when we continually behold Jesus, God transforms us to think and love like Jesus by serving people rather than using them for sinful satisfaction.

God Changes Us

We are told that by beholding the glory of Jesus, we "are being transformed." This miraculous metamorphosis is not something we can do for ourselves; it is possible only by God's doing. Like a skilled potter, the Father conforms us into the image of his Son by enabling us to behold his glory (Isa. 64:8).

Change Is Gradual

Our "beholding" and "being transformed" are both continual, ongoing realities.[1] God does not change us all at once. We continually look, and God continually changes us. By beholding Jesus over time our faith is strengthened, our fight is empowered, temptation becomes less desirable, and our perseverance is fueled. However, this change from one degree of glory to another often happens at a painfully slow pace. It is often a moment-by-moment, day-by-day, week-by-week struggle, but God has promised to complete the work and make us like Jesus (Phil. 1:6).

Seeing Leads to Growing

God has filled the world with living illustrations for our instruction. One such example is found in the way sunflowers grow to maturity. At dawn a young sunflower faces east, awaiting the sun. Throughout the day, the flower's bud follows the sun across the sky, until it sets in the west. At night the flower instinctively resets its face eastward, anticipating the sun's rising in the morning. By continually fixing its gaze upon the sun, the flower reaches maturity.

Believers grow in maturity in a strikingly similar way. Though we cannot see the Son of God physically, we turn the eyes of our heart toward him in faith and behold him in the Scriptures by the power of the Holy Spirit.[2] By reading and meditating upon God's

---

1 Both verbs, "beholding" and "being transformed," are in the present tense.
2 We should also be clear about what it doesn't mean to behold Jesus. *We do not behold Jesus physically.* Let us not forget that many saw Jesus while he walked the earth, but still loved

word through faith we stretch the eyes of our heart to see Jesus's beauty. The word serves as a window through which we behold the glory of Jesus and are transformed into his image. Or as one pastor explained, "Scripture is our only blueprint of the glory of Christ. Only *in* Scripture and only *by* faith can we behold the glory of Christ."[3]

Cultivating a heart that delights in Jesus's glory rather than sin is a lifelong pursuit. But before we can see Jesus rightly, we must recognize what hinders us from beholding him truly.

Sin Hinders Seeing

If it is true that "blessed are the pure in heart for they shall see God," then the opposite is also true—cursed are the impure in heart for they shall not see God. Apart from his saving grace, we are spiritually dead and blindly walk in ways that dishonor God and ultimately destroy us (Eph. 2:1–5). Satan blinds unbelievers from seeing the glory of Christ, and after conversion he attempts to callous believers' hearts with sinful compromises. He aims to seduce us with counterfeit pleasures that deaden our hearts and make us disinterested in glory (2 Cor. 4:4; 11:3).

Most of us think too lightly of our sin. We give little thought to God's name being blasphemed because of us. We are not moved when he says, "You have burdened me with your sins; / you have wearied me with your iniquities" (Isa. 43:24). If we are honest, we are often more concerned about feeling guilty for our sin than

---

their sins. *We do not behold Jesus through images.* The second commandment warns us against looking to images that can only distort who Jesus is and are unable to nurture the faith needed to kill sin. *We do not behold Jesus through visions or dreams.* Miraculous interventions by God can be prayed for, but aren't necessary to grow in holiness.

3 John Owen, *The Glory of Christ* (Edinburgh, UK: Banner of Truth, 1994), 122.

God being grieved by our sin. Our thinking about sin is too often horizontal (how it affects me or other people) and too rarely vertical (what God thinks about it). The Scriptures warn us that this sort of worldly grief leads only to death because it hinders us from being convicted of the godly grief that gives life (2 Cor. 7:10).

What does it reveal about you when you do things before an all-seeing God that you would never do before another person?

Do you ever consider that God sees what you do in the darkness and is grieved by it? Not only is God grieved by our sin, but he is also dragged into it. To a church calloused to their sexual sin, Paul wrote these shocking words, "Do you not know that your bodies are members of Christ? Shall I then take the members of Christ and make them members of a prostitute?" (1 Cor. 6:15). When we go into sin, we do not go alone.

In some sense, when you look at pornography or join your body with a forbidden lover, you unite Jesus with your sin. What a horrific thought. Jesus shed his blood to make us his own, but then we use our bodies to indulge the very sin from which he suffered to save us. By indulging in immoral pleasures, we turn the temple of the Holy Spirit into a palace of perversion.[4]

Many of us are tricked into ignoring the gravity of our sin. Listen to these sobering words to believers:

> Sexual immorality and all impurity or covetousness must not even be named among you, as is proper among saints. . . . For you may be sure of this, that everyone who is sexually immoral or impure, or who is covetous (that is, an idolater), has no inheritance in the kingdom of Christ and God. Let no one deceive

---

4 I am in no way suggesting that Jesus or the Holy Spirit sin in or through our sinning.

you with empty words, for because of these things the wrath of God comes upon the sons of disobedience. (Eph. 5:3–6)

Sin will assure us that we do not need to be moved by God's severe warnings. It will suggest they apply to others and that we are somehow exempt. Friend, please hear this: *if your theology provides you comfort in sin that grieves God, you have a false theology.* Our sin grieves God, and it ought to grieve us as well. God's people must never be apathetic toward their sin. Peter wept bitterly after he denied the Lord (Luke 22:62). Ezra mourned over immorality (Ezra 9:3–5). The sinful woman washed Jesus's feet with her tears (Luke 7:36–50). And what better example is there than David who, after his adultery and murder, prayed, "against you, you only, have I sinned / and done what is evil in your sight" (Ps. 51:4)? David severely sinned against others, but he knew his sin was chiefly against God.

Do you mourn your sin against God? Does your sin shock you anymore?

When we are least mindful of God, we are most susceptible to temptation. When our hearts are cold, we treat "small sins" as inconsequential. Yet after the rush of every perverted click, every adulterous kiss, and every instance of compromise, do you not feel regret? When you yield to the sin from which you should flee, do you not feel shame, as if "your sins have kept good from you" (Jer. 5:25)?

How terrifying to not recognize our danger. Though our sins separate us from God, we assume we can quickly draw near to him, as if we are in control. Yet our sin makes the Scriptures seem insufficient and irrelevant. We cannot snap ourselves back. Prayer feels powerless. We cannot wake ourselves up. Church feels pointless.

Other believers annoy us, and conversations about God feel judg-mental. We fail to sense the danger of the transgression, constricting like serpents around our throats, because our hearts are hardening to the voice of God, perhaps nearer to hell than to heaven.[5]

We need God's intervention to show us his holiness so we can cry along with Isaiah, "Woe is me! For I am lost; for I am a man of unclean lips, and I dwell in the midst of a people of unclean lips; for my eyes have seen the King, the LORD of hosts!" (Isa. 6:5). When we see God's holiness, it exposes our sinfulness—and drives us to Jesus. And this is the key because seeing God is the promise for the pure in heart and *the means by which our hearts are purified.*

Seeing God's holiness and our sinfulness awakens our need for his grace and drives us to Jesus to provide it. Over time, God's grace becomes increasingly precious and sin increasingly repulsive. This is a miraculous work that only God can bring about. Praise God that he delights in doing it.

Seeing through Losing

Before Job's world became a nightmare, he was an enviable man. He was rich, famous, powerful, and yet remained faithful to God. Out of nowhere, everything was turned upside down. Through two rounds of satanic attack, his livestock were pillaged, his servants were slain, his children were crushed to death, and his body was reduced to a sore-infested lump. Job lost everything. The months that followed were filled with "friends" poking him with endless questions about his sin.

---

5 I am not suggesting that believers can lose their salvation. I am saying that comfort with sin should terrify us. The warnings in the book of Hebrews are given to a church that has shown signs of being hardened against God's voice and willing to forsake Jesus for fleeting pleasures (Heb. 2:1–4; 3:7–4:13; 5:11–6:20; 10:26–39; 12:25–29).

Pain screamed loudly, yet God remained silent. Then one day the sky filled with clouds and God drew near and spoke to Job. At no point did God give Job an explanation, but instead revealed his character and power through a list of seemingly endless questions. The questions exposed Job's feelings of entitlement to be treated better than he was. He felt he had deserved something different from God. But Job learned that God is above us and his ways are higher than ours.

After all the questioning from God, Job made a profound statement, "I had heard of you by the hearing of the ear, / but now my eye sees you" (Job 42:5). Job saw God through God's verbal revelation. Through Job's sufferings, God revealed himself to Job in a way that would not have been possible otherwise. Job realized that seeing God was the treasure that made all other earthly treasures pale in comparison.

Would you be willing to lose everything in order to see God more clearly?

Be slow to answer this question. If you are hasty to say, "Yes, of course!" you may not have considered the cost. Seeing God will require you to surrender your beloved sin, your comfort, your reputation, and perhaps much more.

But if you are hesitant to say, "Yes, Lord, do whatever it takes to make me holy," you must also be careful. What is so precious to you that you will not surrender it to God? What idol is so dear to you? Plead with God to show you the glory of Christ as a surpassing treasure. You will never know joy and peace until you surrender.

In the battle for purity, beholding God is at stake. Our adversary would have us do anything but look to Jesus. At times temptation feels inescapable. Yet God shines a promise into the darkness, assuring us of a "way of escape, that you may be able to endure it"

(1 Cor. 10:13). What is this way of escape? By faith, we *look to Jesus* in the Scriptures by the power of the Holy Spirit.

A beloved sister in Christ named Sophia lost much to see God. She began following Jesus in college and is now in her late thirties. She deeply desires to be married, but God has not given her a husband. She knows that God is not torturing her, but at times she feels like he might be.

Her abiding temptation is that men at work come on to her constantly. They are not believers, but they do what Christian men have not done—they pursue her. Her bitterness toward Christian brothers and frustration with her situation shows itself in a battle that rages within her. She longs for companionship, and her passions can feel out of control.

One night she receives a text from a coworker, asking her to go out for drinks. She wants to go, but knows that she is weak and will not be able to resist his advances. *How does Sophia look to Jesus and find his strengthening help?* She needs something more compelling than the thrill of a lover's embrace and more powerful than sin's seductive invitation. She needs something more captivating, more fulfilling, more real than her feelings. She needs to see Jesus. She texts a friend to pray and then in faith grabs her Bible and cries out, "God give me eyes to see Jesus!" She confesses how stupid she feels holding the Bible at a time like this but fights past it. She opens to Matthew's Gospel.[6]

There she finds Peter and the disciples being ravaged by the storm. She sees herself in Peter's shoes as she reads aloud, "'Lord, if it is you, command me to come to you on the water.' [Jesus] said, 'Come.' So Peter got out of the boat and walked on the water and came to Jesus. But when he saw the wind, he was afraid, and

---

6 For more on how we need Christian community in the heat of battle, see chapter 7.

beginning to sink he cried out, 'Lord, save me.' Jesus immediately reached out his hand and took hold of him, saying 'O you of little faith, why did you doubt?'" (Matt. 14:28–31).

Sophia cries out in honest prayer, "Lord, help me to see! I am surrounded by a storm of temptation. I know it is better to be near to Jesus, but I am so weak. I am trying to walk by faith, but I am sinking in my doubt. I want to go with my coworker. I am weak right now. Lord Jesus, reach out your hand and save me."

By looking, speaking, and listening to Jesus, the power of sin slowly lessens and Sophia sees the temptation for what it is, a path to sorrow. She knows that God would be grieved if she sinned with her coworker and that she would mar her witness for Christ. Beholding Jesus as the ever-present Savior for sinking sinners gives Sophia strength to worship God by resisting sin.

Glory on the Horizon

I have been in the heat of battle many times, and I know as well as you do that simply reading a few verses does not magically kill temptation. That's nonsense. Bible reading is not like popping a pill or chugging a spiritual espresso. We are in the midst of a spiritual battle.

Satan provoked Sophia's flesh with lustful promises, but she fought back by reaching out and grasping Christ in faith by the Spirit through the word. Learning to put our sinful flesh to death by the sword of Scripture is essential in the Christian life (Rom. 8:13). The latter part of this book is dedicated to developing how we grow in beholding Christ, but let's conclude with these two reminders.

1. Seeing God Happens over Time

The sort of faith-filled fighting Sophia exhibited was the fruit of many years of learning to see God. She has not always obeyed God, but she is not the same person she was three years ago. She has grown in spiritual strength by daily seeking God through his word. She has grown in confessing and repenting when she compromises and walking in the good news that God still loves her.

This is why believers read the Bible regularly. Jesus assured us that we need it more than we need food (Matt. 4:4). As we come to the word in faith, we behold God's glory. Lust becomes less lovely. Apathy turns to holy passion. Cravings are overtaken by contentment. The transformation from one degree of glory to another is slow, yet certain.[7]

Beholding strengthens our believing which fuels our obeying. As we strive in faith by the power of the Spirit, God's word cuts out the cancer of abiding sin and makes us more like him (Heb. 4:12). So look, and keep looking to Jesus.

2. Set Your Hope on Seeing Christ

On a day not far from now, the Lord Jesus will arise from the Father's right hand and descend from glory with a myriad of angels and countless numbers of the redeemed. He will transform our bodies to share in his glory, and we will be ushered into the place he has prepared for us. We will no longer know temptation or sin, for nothing impure will enter that land. Instead, we will forever behold the face of the Father, the source of unfathomable love and joy (Rev. 22:4).

Setting our hope on the glories of Jesus's promised return has purifying power for us while we wait: "Beloved, we are God's children now, and what we will be has not yet appeared; but we know that when he appears we shall be like him, because we shall see him

---

7 Chapter 7 is dedicated to helping us think about how to cultivate heavenly affections.

42

as he is. And everyone who thus hopes in him purifies himself as he is pure" (1 John 3:2–3).

The fast-approaching return of Jesus is the substance of our encouragement and guards us from the deceitfulness of sin (Heb. 3:13). It gives us courage to pursue relationships in which we confess sins quickly, honestly, and regularly. Over time, it becomes the joy of our heart in such a way that we treasure Jesus over the passing pleasures of sin.

Do you regularly set your hope on Jesus's return? If not, might it be because you love this present life too much?

Jesus's final prayer before he was betrayed and crucified was for us to see his glory: "Father, I desire that they also, whom you have given me, may be with me where I am, to see my glory that you have given me because you loved me before the foundation of the world" (John 17:24).

May God make his desire our desire as well.

3

Passion

"Let your fountain be blessed,
and rejoice in the wife of your youth,
a lovely deer, a graceful doe.
Let her breasts fill you at all times with delight;
be intoxicated always in her love."

PROVERBS 5:18–19

SEX IS LIKE FIRE. When fire is kept in a fireplace, it provides light, beauty, and warmth in a home. But if the flames escape, it will burn down the house.[1] Sex is wonderfully powerful. Yet enjoying it without instruction will lead to destruction. This is why God is so careful to explain both why he created sex and how we should enjoy it.

Sex with a Purpose

There is a difference between pure sex and perverted sex. Sadly, many of us have known only the perverted version. The world

1　I first heard this illustration from Tommy Nelson in his teaching on Song of Solomon in 1991.

teaches us the way of the harlot in Proverbs, who "eats and wipes her mouth / and says, 'I have done no wrong'" (Prov. 30:20). Sex is popularly portrayed as a means to satisfy a physical appetite, not as a divinely designed gift. Rather than being "naked and unashamed" (Gen. 2:25) like Adam and Eve in the garden, sexual experience is marred by selfish indulgence, affectionless enjoyment, haunting guilt, and inescapable shame.

But God has something better for us.

God does not blush when he speaks about intimacy or orgasms. He designed our bodies with parts that actually become one, in the most intimate and enjoyable way imaginable, to produce new life. He could have made us to reproduce by laying eggs or shedding cells. But instead, he chose to produce life through sexual intimacy. But procreation isn't even the most amazing aim of sex. God uses the one-flesh union of a husband and wife in marriage as a picture of his exclusive love for his people.[2] He has brought his people to himself and committed to love, serve, protect, and care for them in the context of intimate, secure, covenantal love. We enjoy God, and in a mysterious way, he enjoys us such that he unites us with himself and sings over us in glory.[3]

Pure sex occurs when a husband and wife willingly join their bodies to become one flesh, reflecting Jesus's union with the church.[4] A husband giving himself in sexual union mirrors Christ giving himself in spiritual union. Likewise, a wife giving herself in sexual

2   See Isa. 54:5; Ezek. 16; Hos. 1:2, 9:1; John 3:29; 1 Cor. 6:15–20; Eph. 5:22–33; Rev. 19:7.

3   Isa. 62:5; Zeph. 3:17; 1 Cor. 6:17.

4   Many Jewish interpreters have viewed Song of Solomon as an allegory portraying Yahweh as the lover and the woman as Israel, and many in church history have taken the lover as Christ the bridegroom and the woman as his bride, the church.

union reflects the church giving herself to Christ in spiritual union. Sex should cause us to marvel at Jesus because all its pleasures point to the glorious one who made them. But sin perverts God's good design and can even make it seem strange.

Several years ago my family and I walked through a carnival's house of mirrors. The walls were lined with mirrors designed to twist our reflection and present a distorted image. Some stretched us to look tall and thin; others rendered us short and tubby. Everywhere we walked, things looked right in some ways, and strange in other ways.

Our fallen world is a house of mirrors that distorts everything, including sexuality. I recently saw a condom commercial that declared, "Sex is the sandwich; you can put whatever you want on it."[5] That's the world's take on sex. Sex is whatever you want it to be, because, well, it's all about you. Sex can be recreational or relational—whenever, however, and with whomever you want it. But this perversion of God's purpose has devastating effects. Sin twists our perception of sex in such a way that it maintains aspects of its good design, while drastically distorting others. *Perverted sex*, therefore, is any sexual engagement outside the union of a husband and wife in marriage. This means that sex outside of marriage, sexually pleasing yourself, and watching others have sex are all perversions that rob us of God's good design.[6]

In 1 Corinthians 6:15–18, the apostle Paul presents a graphic description of how sin twists God's intent for sex:

5   Trojan condom ad, 2018.

6   God has established marriage as the uniting of one man and one woman in an exclusive covenant commitment for a lifetime. Though some attempt to redefine marriage, humans do not have the authority to do so, because marriage is not our idea. Marriage is God's institution. Any other union, therefore, is a perversion of God's design and isn't marriage at all.

Do you not know that your bodies are members of Christ? Shall I then take the members of Christ and make them members of a prostitute? Never! Or do you not know that he who is joined to a prostitute becomes one body with her? For, as it is written, "The two will become one flesh." But he who is joined to the Lord becomes one spirit with him. Flee from sexual immorality. Every other sin a person commits is outside the body, but the sexually immoral person sins against his own body.

Our body was designed to be a temple in which the Holy Spirit dwells. The Spirit joins believers with Christ, making us members of his body. But when a believer sins sexually, we turn the temple of God's Spirit into a house of idolatry. Using your body for pure sex is an act of worship, but perverted sex unites your Spirit-indwelled body to another's in a way that uniquely offends God and harms you.

Sexual sin is also a sin against the person you have sex with, even if it's consensual. How can I say that? Because love never does anything to harm another person's relationship with God. For instance, sex outside marriage is not an act of true love. God's word warns us that defiling the marriage bed incurs his judgment (Heb. 13:4). True love wouldn't lead someone toward judgment; it would help him or her toward true joy. Lust is a self-serving sin that uses others for selfish delight, always at the cost of their relationship with God. Love, however, is oriented toward enjoying someone else in the way God designed.

But Satan's temptations attack God's good purposes. Pornography twists the portrait of God's exclusive, intimate faithfulness into an exhibition of selfish indulgence without care for those it uses. The hook-up culture of one-night stands and open marriages mars the picture of God's committed love. Masturbation and the fantasy world of "romance" novels scoff at the call to serve others during sex. Homosexual relationships distort the relationship between Christ and his church. Satan knows sex is designed to promote God's glory—which is why he wars so diligently to destroy it.

Sex for Pleasure

Try not to blush as you listen to the inspired words of these married lovers:

> Let him kiss me with the kisses of his mouth! . . . He has brought me into his chambers. . . . His left hand is under my head and his right hand embraces me! . . . Your eyes are doves behind your veil . . . hair . . . teeth . . . lips . . . cheeks . . . neck . . . breast. . . . You are altogether beautiful, my love. . . . You have captivated my heart with one glance of your eyes. . . . Much better is your love than wine. . . . Your lips drip nectar . . . honey and milk are under your tongue. . . . I came to my bride . . . I gathered . . . I ate . . . I drank. . . . Be drunk with love. (Song 1–5)

Why would God invite us to listen in to such an intimate conversation? Because God wants us to know he gave us sex to be wonderfully pleasurable.

Have you ever considered that God designed the male and female reproductive organs, with thousands of sensory nerves, specifically to enable husbands and wives to pleasure each other? He made the orgasm exhilarating so spouses could celebrate their closeness in a most intimate and enthralling way. God hardwired us with the capacity for attraction, arousal, and satisfaction. Though intimacy and orgasms can be enjoyed apart from knowing God, pleasure's fullest measure is experienced when we know that sex is made for more than satisfying physical desires.

In one sense, pleasurable sex is a risky invention by God. People could (as we often do) decide that we want to enjoy the gift and neglect the giver. If sex weren't pleasurable, one could argue, there would be a whole lot less sin in the world. So why would God make sex enjoyable? Because pleasure-giving gifts are a reflection of his very nature.[7] He is a benevolent, joyful, creative God who made a world filled with delights both public (like sunsets) and intimate (like sex).

We ought to be amazed that God uses his creativity for our pleasure. He made good-tasting food and vividly colored creation so we would marvel at him—and he did the same with sex. He created it to be pleasurable so we would find pleasure in him. Sexual enjoyment is enhanced when accompanied by thankfulness to the one who designed it. Intimacy is enriched when we learn that its purpose isn't mindless passion, but soul-knitting expression of covenant love that protects us from satanic attack (1 Cor. 7:5).

A perverted view of sex, meanwhile, tempts us to see intimacy merely as a means of receiving pleasure. But God designed sexual intimacy as an opportunity to serve our spouse. Sex is about giving pleasure to another, not just taking pleasure for ourselves. We don't use others to satisfy our fantasies, but to learn to patiently pursue and sacrificially care for the needs of the spouse God has given to us. We give of ourselves for their pleasure in a way that reflects God's giving of himself for our pleasure.

Sexual pleasure, as all other pleasures, is intended to serve as a foretaste of the eternal pleasure we will enjoy with God. In Psalm

---

7   The Scriptures assure us that God both gives pleasure to us (Pss. 16:11; 36:8; Matt. 25:21) and receives pleasure in what he does for us (Ps. 147:11; Hag. 1:8; Luke 12:32; Phil. 2:13).

16:11 David prayed, "In your presence there is fullness of joy; / at your right hand are pleasures forevermore." Every bit of pleasure we experience in this life—including sexual pleasure—is meant to serve our souls by pointing to a final day when we'll experience the uninterrupted pleasure of God's presence.

Can you see that God gives us commands because he wants something *for* us not just something *from* us? Can you see that God's call to purity is aimed at giving pleasure rather than withholding it? Can you see how it's designed to point to his benevolence? Can you see how beholding God's benevolence can help you resist the temptation to settle for fleeting pleasures?

Sex Has Power

Have you ever played with a set of magnets? When their poles face a certain way, they attract each other. Depending on their strength, magnets can be nearly impossible to pull apart. In a similar way, God has designed sex to have a magnetic effect. Sex is designed to unite people, not just physically but spiritually. This power can serve as a blessing or seem like a curse.

When our sinful flesh is in control, the desire for sexual fulfillment can tempt us to do all sorts of senseless things to satisfy it. Many people devote obscene amounts of time, energy, and money trying to get it. People spend hours chasing the mirage of pleasure through pornography. Others destroy their careers and families through adulterous affairs. Even born-again children of God, when not walking by the Spirit, can be overcome by the urges of passion.

Sex is so powerful that we cannot have it without consequence. It's designed to knit souls and intertwine emotions in an inseparable way (Mal. 2:15). When sex unites a husband and wife, it is a blessing that solidifies their covenant love. When sex is misused, however, it harms us. Sometimes we don't feel harmed immediately, but eventually the harm will become evident. One young man who occasionally hooks up with other men through a social-media app explained, "I'm lonely, so I chat. Then we meet up. When it's happening, I feel affirmed, desired, and special. But every time it's over, I feel numb and insecure and more empty than before it began."

Many of us know such sorrow all too well. The wounds left by broken relationships haunt us. Guilt, shame, regret, and emptiness are but a few of the feelings left in the wake of misused sex. This is why rape is not just another crime; it's a most heinous violation that steals something sacred. And this is why adultery isn't like other marital offenses; it wounds in a crushingly intimate way.

This is also why sex is such an important gift to married couples. It acts as a magnet that unites their souls in an ever-deepening way. Several years ago my friend John met with a group of young men. He was the only married man at the time, and the rest were dabbling with pornography. In a moment of brutal honesty, one of them said to John, "I just don't understand how you can have sex with the same woman all the time. That seems boring." John replied, "You're assuming I have sex with the same woman all the time."

Their silent stares begged for explanation.

John explained how his wife is not the same woman he married. She is always growing and changing as a woman, as he is always growing and changing as a man. They are not the same people as the day they got married, and neither is their sexual intimacy. Like a fine wine, their intimacy has matured over time. The flames of physical and emotional passion were a part, but not the whole, and their appreciation for the joys of sexual union have broadened and deepened year after year.

John explained that by continually neglecting God's good design for sex, his friends were settling for flashes of sinful passion instead of the white-hot coals of enduring intimacy. God designed sex to be best enjoyed when based on something other than appearance or performance. He bases it on committed love that reflects his unending love for all who trust in Christ.

This is where power and pleasure should be considered together. The world portrays pleasure as flash-in-the-pan passion that moves from lover to lover and fantasy to fantasy, as if novelty and variety deliver real pleasure. But such "pleasure" never fulfills; it only dishonors our Maker, harms our consciences, deepens our discontent, and corrupts our relationships. What man can click on a pornographic picture, stop, and be satisfied? What woman can fantasize for a few seconds, stop, and be satisfied? Sin pulls us with the promise of pleasure; it leaves us parched, pursuing a mirage of water.

God summons us to believe his promises about the power and pleasure of sex. I'm not implying he promises that sex will always be enjoyable or easy for married couples. Because marriage is the union of an ever-changing and ever-growing pair of broken people, we can expect sexual intimacy to have seasons both sour and sweet. And this is not unusual; it's part of God's wise design. Sex is a bond between a husband and wife that strengthens over time. Married couples make love on their honeymoon and after a miscarriage. They make love to conceive children and after they bury them. They make love when bodies are healthy and during battles against cancer. As a husband and wife pursue each other through intimate service, sacrifice, and struggle—God blesses them in a way the world can never know.

God ordains lovemaking for couples when we are richer or poorer, in sickness and in health, when life is better or worse, until death do we part because it reflects his own enduring love for us.

This is where those of us who consider sex either terrifying or uninteresting should pause and reflect. The word of God is clear: just as it's wrong to engage in sexual activity outside of marriage, it's also wrong to *not* engage in it if you are married (1 Cor. 7:5).[8] But God does not design things this way because he's mean or uncaring. In his wisdom, he's prescribed a way for husbands and wives to become vulnerable in the most intimate way. Yes, there will be need for prayer and planning and counsel through challenging seasons, but God will use that process to help you look to him for grace in your time of need. After all, it is only by looking to him that you can find the true purpose, pleasure, and power of sex.

God Is Better Than Sex

Surely it's possible to read this chapter and get discouraged. If you are single, or same-sex attracted, or committed to celibacy, or in a marriage where sex is virtually nonexistent, you may find this all a bit torturous. Remember, though, that *your fulfillment as a person is not dependent on being sexually or romantically fulfilled.* Jesus was never married, never romantically involved, and never enjoyed sex. And yet he was the most joyful and complete person who has ever lived.

Now you might think, *Yeah, thanks buddy, but I'm not Jesus.* I get it. But please hear this: sexual pleasure will never ultimately satisfy you. A wonderful spouse will never fulfill you. Neither sex nor spouse can do what only God can. You can have the best spouse on the planet and enjoy the most fulfilling sex life imaginable, yet this

8 If you and your spouse are facing challenges with sexual intimacy, please reach out to a spiritually mature couple, a trusted pastor, or a godly biblical counselor. It may feel shameful or embarrassing to discuss such intimate details of your life, but God desires to help you, and he often uses others to do so.

fact remains: if your heart is not satisfied in God, it will wander to find satisfaction elsewhere. Spouses can be wonderful helpers, but they are sorry saviors. Jesus alone can satisfy something as complex as the human soul.

The ultimate goal of sex isn't just enjoying your spouse; it's enjoying the giver himself. God is better than the best sex. We know this because we will live forever on a new earth—without our present experience of marriage or sex—and yet will experience pleasures forevermore.[9]

We pursue sexual purity to get a glimpse of the God who loves us. As we fight against wrong views of sexual desire, we see ever more clearly a good God who gives good gifts. And this helps us to trust him in every area of our life, for we know his love is what our hearts were designed to enjoy.

9 Matt. 22:30; Ps. 16; Isa. 51:11; Rev. 21–22.

4

Enemies

IN JOHN BUNYAN'S *PILGRIM'S PROGRESS*, a man named Christian flees the City of Destruction in hopes of reaching the Celestial City. Every sort of adversity confronts him, but he presses on by clinging to God's promises. During his pilgrimage, Christian and his friend, Faithful, venture upon a city known as Vanity.

Vanity is a city that never sleeps. As Bunyan tells it, the architect of the ancient metropolis was Satan. He designed the city as an unavoidable obstacle for heaven-bound travelers. Like a spider's web, its design is to ensnare pilgrims as they pass through.

In the center of the city is a fair that never closes. Like a porch light that draws bugs on a summer night, the sights, sounds, and smells of Vanity Fair enchant travelers. Pleasures of every sort are on offer. But the residents find believers in God scandalous, since they claim to walk according to truth. Eventually a mob surrounds these pilgrims, hurling insults and dragging away Faithful to be burned.

Vanity Fair's unspoken motto, "conform or die," is alive and well today. As we travel heavenward, we too face opposition—always present, though not always visible. Mighty forces are within us, around us, and behind us. The Bible calls these opponents the flesh, the world, and the devil (Eph. 2:1–3).

The Enemy within Us: Our Flesh

For as long as Kasey could remember, she had loved God. Songs about heaven warmed her heart, and Bible stories comforted her soul. She believed Jesus was God's Son and had died for her. Yet for Kasey, this did not make life simple or easy.

In elementary school she sensed being different from other girls. She used to secretly dress up and pretend she was a boy because it felt natural to her. As she matured, friendly companionship with other girls often became overwhelming and blurred with romantic fascination. On one occasion she and her best female friend secretly explored their affection, leaving her plagued with shame.

Kasey knew her same-sex desires were not in line with God's design, which only stirred haunting questions: *What is wrong with me? Why did God make me this way? If I love God, why don't these feelings just go away? How can I fix my feelings? Is God's word really telling me the truth? Am I really a Christian?*

Of all the battles we fight as Christians, the most difficult and enduring tends to be the battle *within*. This can be confusing. It was for Kasey. Though God's Spirit produces love for him and hatred for sin, our flesh loves sin and has no love for God. From the moment we come to faith in Jesus, we enter this daily conflict; and as the days add up, it can produce weariness, doubt, and grief. Kasey felt every ounce of it.

The apostle Paul could genuinely sympathize with her struggle:

I do not understand my own actions. For I do not do what I want, but I do the very thing I hate. . . . For I have the desire to do what

is right, but not the ability to carry it out. For I do not do the good
I want, but the evil I do not want is what I keep on doing. . . .
Wretched man that I am! Who will deliver me from this body
of death? (Rom. 7:15–19, 24)

When we become disciples of Jesus, we are given new hearts to
love God. The Holy Spirit indwells us in order to conform us to
Christ. He gives us the mind of Christ, so that we desire, think,
and feel as he does (1 Cor. 2:6–16).

But our flesh, or sinful nature, violently resists this change.

Our flesh acts like a magnet toward sin. It loves the world of Vanity
Fair. It loves pleasure above all. It goes to war within our bodies. As we
meander through our Vanity Fair, we feel attracted to the sins abound-
ing in it. Not everyone feels it the same way, but everyone feels it.

Everyone's flesh is weak toward particular sins. That is, we each
wrestle with some temptations more than others. We need to know this
about ourselves. It helps, then, to identify our specific areas of weakness.
For what does your flesh hunger? Anonymous sexual encounters? Pornographic escapes? A lover more exciting than your spouse? Intimacy
outside marriage? Or maybe sexual sin isn't really your struggle. How
does your flesh respond to those who do? Do you feel judgmental?
Are you impatient with others' weaknesses? Do you have difficulty
discerning your own sin? None of us is immune to our inner enemy.

Sometimes our sin is awakened and strengthened. Other times
it seems to be sleeping. But it is never dead. This traitor inside the
gates of your heart is always, subtly or with screaming voice, woo-
ing you away from devotion for God.[1]

1   John Owen, *Indwelling Sin*, in *Overcoming Sin and Temptation*, ed. Kelly Kapic and Justin
    Taylor (Wheaton, IL: Crossway, 2015), 274–75.

The Enemy around Us: The World

Years ago I watched a documentary featuring a bizarre flower called the pitcher plant. The petals are vibrant with color and its cup emanates a sweet aroma that attracts bugs. A camera captured the ominous journey of one bug drawn to the scent. It lands on the edge of the flower and slowly ventures past hair-like spokes that line the spiral stem. Unbeknownst to the bug, the spokes it presses past are inflexible barbs, trapping and dooming him to be devoured by the plant's digestive juices, disguised as sweet-smelling nectar.

The term *world* has several meanings in Scripture, but a major one is this: a Satan-inspired system that caters to fleshly cravings by promising fulfillment apart from God. Like the pitcher plant, the world radiates images and ideas that serve our sinful desires. The world aggressively markets sin. It assures great pleasures, but hides the price tag. It denounces what God glorifies and glamorizes what God denounces.

Shortly after I became a believer, I recognized this world system for the first time. As I watched a show, I realized there was a message behind everything on the screen. I was promised respect if I get a new car; safety if I invest in a certain insurance policy; happiness if I eat the right burger. But one thing was glaringly absent: God. No commercial broke through the entertainment to say, "Here's your friendly reminder that one day soon, you'll stand before a holy God and give account for everything you've ever done—so turn to Jesus." The aim of this world system is to set your heart, hope, and trust on anything but God.

Satan has corrupted every sphere of life. He has infiltrated entertainment, technology, politics, economics, education, and many religions, all with the aim of knitting hearts to worldly wisdom and pleasure. The world declares that life apart from God is not only possible, but profitable. This is why the apostle John warned: "Do not love the world or the things in the world. If anyone loves the world, the love of the Father is not in him. For all that is in the world—the desires of the flesh and the desires of the eyes and pride of life—is not from the Father but is from the world" (1 John 2:15–16).

None of this means we ought to see everything on earth as evil. We must, however, understand that everything we read, see, hear, taste, and touch is affected by the fall. The world is designed to distract our hearts, distort the truth, and dull any desire to delight in God. The world is, in a sense, evangelistic. Like the flower, it gives off an alluring aroma—and then traps you with barbs of conformity. Following Jesus is not easy in this fallen world system.

The Enemy Who Stalks Us: The Devil

I was awakened during the middle of the night. The darkness I sensed was smothering. Breathing was difficult. It felt as if something were sitting on my chest, grasping my throat. Paralyzing fear kept me from speaking or moving. Eventually I said the name "Jesus" and began to faintly sing the words of a familiar hymn. This put a quick end to my experience, but it left a lasting impression.

Spiritual warfare is normally experienced in subtler ways, but it is no less real. God warns us that we battle "spiritual forces of evil" and have an unseen enemy who "prowls around like a roaring lion seeking someone to devour" (Eph. 6:12; 1 Pet. 5:8). Be certain of this: the battle for purity is fundamentally spiritual. All Satan's efforts have a single aim: to destroy you. Whether Adam, Eve, Job, Judas, Peter, Jesus, the church, or you, his goal is the same. Remember this the next time you're tempted. The inviting voice is not from a friend, but a sinister foe.

But Satan is patient in his attempts to destroy you. Dietrich Bonhoeffer brilliantly describes his approach:

> Satan does not here fill us with hatred of God, but with forgetfulness of God. . . . The lust thus aroused envelops the mind and . . . the powers of clear discrimination and of decision are taken from us. The questions present themselves: *Is what the flesh desires really sin in this case?* . . . It is here that everything within me rises up against the Word of God.[2]

Satan wants you to distrust God's word and to disbelieve his promises. He wants you to see what God calls evil as being good for you. He wants you to see indulgence as freedom and restraint as slavery. Though he prowls like a lion, Satan often wears the disguise of a harmless sheep or dazzling angel. Satan poses as a friend, but, like Judas, will betray you with a kiss. He is the thief who comes to steal your joy, kill your fellowship with God, and destroy your soul.[3]

The devil's work against us comes in two basic forms: *alluring* and *accusing*.[4]

Satan Allures

Satan serves as the tour guide of Vanity Fair. Suggestions of pleasure are intertwined with truth and lies. He offers a cup of promised

2 Dietrich Bonhoeffer, *Temptation* (London: SCM Press, 1961), 33. Emphasis added.
3 Matt. 7:15; John 10:10; 2 Cor. 11:14.
4 I should clarify at this point that Satan has likely never tempted any of us personally. He is not present everywhere like God. Yet, he is called the god of this world and the prince who commissions demonic forces to labor diligently against us. When we speak of Satan tempting us, we should understand it as him tempting our flesh through the world, most normally with the help of his demonic minions.

refreshment, but doesn't disclose the drop of poison within. He is a master counterfeiter, assuring you that compromise will not kill; you can escape any time you like.

Like a fisherman who presents the bait and hides the hook, Satan fishes for us with personalized lures.[5] He has studied you and knows what you like, maybe even more than you do. And he knows how and when to present it. He steals the seeds of God's word and plants his own deceptive tares (Matt. 13:25; Luke 8:4–15). As I write this, I have prayed for you to see the specific ways Satan seduces you. I share Paul's concern: "I am afraid that as the serpent deceived Eve by his cunning, your thoughts will be led astray from a sincere and pure devotion to Christ" (2 Cor. 11:3).

Satan desires nothing more than to keep you from seeing Christ. He knows that if we pursue purity, we'll see glimmers of God's beauty and remain alert. So he does all he can to keep your Bible closed, your prayer closet empty, your fellowship shallow, and your trust in God's promises hollow. So the promise in James 4:7 ("Resist the devil, and he will flee from you") cannot be divorced from the warning in Ephesians 4:27 ("Give no opportunity to the devil"). Leave him at Vanity Fair, and press on toward the Celestial City.[6]

Satan Accuses

Since Satan cannot condemn those in Christ, his next best trick is to make us *feel* that we're condemned (Rom. 8:1). Before a sin, Satan tempts you to believe repentance will be easy. After a sin, Satan tempts you to believe repentance is impossible. Arrows of

5   I have borrowed the fishing imagery from Thomas Brooks, *Precious Remedies against Satan's Devices* (Edinburgh, UK, Banner of Truth, 1968), 29.
6   We'll talk about how to do this in part 2, Pathways to Purity.

accusation aim for the heart to empty it of hope. *You are too dirty to be loved*, he whispers. *God is ashamed of you. You will always be a failure.* He is the great accuser, continually dragging believers' failures to their minds and before God's throne (Job 1–2; Rev. 12:10).

Satan labors to confuse conviction with condemnation. When we sin, feelings of guilt and remorse are appropriate. Conviction is when the Holy Spirit alerts us, "Jesus would not look at that. Jesus would not say that. Jesus would not do that with his body. Jesus would not coddle that thought in his mind. There is a way of escape; take it!" (see 1 Cor. 10:13). The Holy Spirit's conviction is a gift that should move us to confession and repentance.

But Satan is a historian. He is the master of replaying old sins to the tune of accusation. He digs up past failures and then blackmails us with reminders of why God is disappointed with us. Before sin, Satan is the tempter who whispers, "You should do this!" After sin, Satan is the accuser who whispers, "How could you have done this!" Satan kills through temptation and then buries with guilt.

But whether he allures with sugar on the tongue or accuses with salt in a wound, the devil is always working. His aim is to turn your gaze from God, because seeing him with sober eyes strengthens your fight for faith in the one greater than all your foes.

Greater Than Your Enemies

Here's the thing: the enemies of purity are too strong for us. We stand no chance against them. But praise be to God that "he who is in you is greater than he who is in the world" (1 John 4:4). The good news for travelers wearied by Vanity Fair is that Jesus has decisively entered the scene. He came to earth and walked through the fair, yet endured the temptations without surrendering to one of them (Matt. 4:1–11; Heb. 4:15). Why, according to the apostle

John, did the Son of God appear? To destroy the works of the devil (1 John 3:8).

On the cross, Jesus was crushed for our sins. The innocent one was condemned for the sins that had condemned us. If you are trusting him, hear this: Jesus was pure in your place. He was crushed for your filth. The certificate listing your failures was nailed to the wood and covered by his blood (Col. 2:13–15).

And after three days in the grave, Jesus rose from the dead. When he came forth, he sealed both our *deliverance* from this evil world and our *hope* for a better world to come. He also gave his Spirit to empower us against our flesh, and promised that nothing, not even the devil, can separate us from divine love (Gal. 1:4; 5:16; Rom. 8:38–39).

So when your sinful flesh pulls, think of Jesus's sinless flesh that was torn for you. When the world invites, consider Jesus, who calls you to heaven. When Satan allures you with temptation, think of Jesus's broken body, given to free you from condemnation. When Satan points to all the reasons you should be condemned, point to Calvary, where a blood-washed slate now declares, "It is finished!"

A day is fast approaching when Jesus will return and the devil will be "thrown into the lake of fire and . . . tormented day and night forever and ever" (Rev. 20:10). On that day, we will be ushered into a new land where sin holds no sway. Until then, look to Christ. He is able to keep you from stumbling as you travel through the trials and temptations of Vanity Fair (Jude 24–25).

5

Fallout

*In Christ, there is no condemnation for sin, but even
forgiven sin can carry devastating consequences.*

ON OUR WEDDING NIGHT my wife and I settled into our hotel suite.
As we sat on the bed, she handed me a well-worn envelope decorated
with colorful hearts. Three words were written on the front: "To The
One." I opened the seal and unfolded the paper to find a letter she
wrote when she was thirteen, to the man she intended to marry. The
letter declared that she had saved herself for this special night.

I wept as I read it. My tears were stirred by the sweetness of her
letter, but also by the sorrow that I couldn't offer the same gift in
return. Sadness invaded that sacred moment. Though I was saved
and secure in the forgiveness of Jesus, I was still haunted by the
ghosts of my past. Though our marriage pleased God and delighted
us, we could not escape the effects of my sin. I did not feel guilt
on that night, but I did feel regret.

When a nuclear bomb explodes in a city, the initial blast levels buildings and incinerates people. The explosion also launches trillions of invisible radioactive particles into the sky. These particles slowly drift back to earth, where the survivors begin to feel the effects, the fallout. In the months and years to follow, many will suffer all kinds of sickness, and sometimes even death.

Like a detonated bomb, sexual sin causes immediate damage, but it does not stop there. Fallout always follows. Many of us know this all too well. The pleasures of sin are shallow, but the pain of the aftermath is deep. At some point the pain hits, like it did on my wedding night. In that moment, I would have traded almost anything to give my bride the same gift she'd given me. But I couldn't. Sin had stolen it.

Personal Fallout

I have seen careers—built on decades of schooling, financial investment, and diligence—ruined by viewing pornography on a work computer. In churches I've attended, friendships were marred and fellowship broken over sexual indiscretion. Who can measure the pain of husbands or wives when at last they discover unfaithfulness in their spouse? Or who can heal the wounds of sexual abuse, which steal the precious innocence of so many? The list could go on, and you could add your own stories, but the point is clear—the consequences of sin, whether done *by* us or *to* us, tend to linger.

Defiling the Temple

Solomon warned his sons about the devastating consequences of sexual sin: "Can a man carry fire next to his chest / and his clothes not be burned" (Prov. 6:27)? The answer is, *Of course not.* What you do with your body has lasting effects.

I once sat with a man as he shared with his fiancée the sorrowful news of an STD he carries, the long-term consequence of a previous lifestyle. Moreover, scientific research is proving that indulgence in porn hinders brain development in adolescents and even changes the adult brain in ways that produce addictive responses. I've counseled newlywed couples struggling with intimacy due to years of masturbation and porn use while they were single. The new frontier of transgender experimentation has already devastated the psychological and physiological health of many. These aren't fearmongering stories; they're reminders that actions have consequences. When we mishandle its pleasures, we harm ourselves.[1]

But the bodily harm goes even deeper. "Flee from sexual immorality," the apostle Paul warned. "Every other sin a person commits is outside the body, but the sexually immoral person sins against his own body. Or do you not know that your body is a temple of the Holy Spirit within you, whom you have from God?" (1 Cor. 6:18–19). Our bodies were built to be temples of praise in which God's Spirit dwells (Rom. 12:1–2; 1 Cor. 6:19–20). Yet when we crowd a sanctuary with idols, we defile it. Sexual sin uniquely dishonors the body because sex unites the bodies of image bearers in a way nothing else does. Uniting your body (which was created *for* God's will) with another person's body (in an act *against* God's will) demeans both bodies (Rom. 1:24, 27). This is why many of

---

1 See Josh McDowell Ministries, *The Porn Phenomenon: The Impact of Pornography in the Digital Age* (The Barna Group and Josh McDowell Ministries, 2016), 91; Peter R Coleman, "Online Porn May Damage Teenage Brains," Coleman Institute for Addiction Medicine website, May 26, 2016, thecolemaninstitute.com/tci-blog/68-online-porn-may-damage -teenage-brains/; Ryan T. Anderson, "Sex Reassignment Doesn't Work. Here Is the Evidence," The Heritage Foundation website, March 9, 2018, www.heritage.org/gender/commentary /sex-reassignment-doesnt-work-here-the-evidence/; Nancy Pearcey, *Love Thy Body* (Grand Rapids, MI: Baker, 2018), 117–54.

us bear grievous scars and haunting memories that we wish would go away.² Indeed, our "body is not meant for sexual immorality, but for the Lord" (1 Cor. 6:13).

Distorting Your Vision

When people are drunk, they are out of touch with reality. They say and do reckless things because their perception of reality is distorted. Sin has a similar effect. I recently spoke with someone who's convinced that watching a popular show containing graphic nudity isn't that big of a deal. I tried to explain how easily we're deceived by the sin we love. When we succumb, we lose spiritual sobriety. Every cup of temptation is served with the ancient whisper, "You will not surely die." The more we sip the potion, then, the more we become disillusioned, and sin appears altogether reasonable. We may convince ourselves that watching sensual shows isn't serious, but Jesus says it is safer to tear out your eye than to lust. *Dating this nonbeliever won't make me forsake Jesus*, we might tell ourselves, but God warns us to take heed lest we fall. *This affair will never be found out*, we can start to think, but Jesus says everything will come into the light (Luke 8:17).

When our spiritual senses grow dull, we justify walking past Scripture's warning signs. Before we know it, we are in quicksand, sinking deeper with each step. The longer we give ourselves to sin, the more we prefer it, and the weaker our resistance becomes. Eventually we become so deceived that we start thinking wrong

2 Victims of sexual abuse experience their trauma in various ways. Feelings of grief, guilt, shame, fear, despair, and rage can haunt every aspect of life. Please know that the grace of Jesus is sufficient to help and heal you from the horrific circumstances you have endured. No one should walk through the aftermath of sexual abuse alone. If you have not already, reach out to a trusted Christian friend and begin the process of healing. Together, you can speak to your pastor and seek professional help.

is right, and right is wrong (Isa. 5:20–21). Just as beholding Jesus purifies our heart (1 John 2:28–3:3), so giving in to sin clouds our heart and pulls us farther from God.

How have you found yourself justifying things Scripture forbids? How would you know if you were being deceived?

Destroying Your Life

I don't remember many chapels from my time in seminary, but one I will never forget. Chuck Swindoll, who served as our chancellor, stepped to the pulpit visibly burdened, carrying a Bible in his hand and a written statement. A pastor from our seminary had fallen into grave sexual sin, disqualified himself from ministry, and destroyed his family. Swindoll preached about the dangers of sin, exhorting us to fight it by imagining the aftermath a fall would cause.[3]

Over the years I've followed his advice, and I'd like to help you do the same. I want to walk you through a scene to see what lies ahead on the path of sin. This is a scenario I've imagined to help me, but I trust it can serve you as well.

Envision yourself calling together your elders and sitting in their midst, telling them how you have betrayed their trust. See their sunken faces and feel their broken hearts.

Listen to them consider how they'll tell the church. Imagine the congregation's confusion and how it will affect those who've heard you say so often that Jesus is better than anything else.

Imagine how the name of Christ will be mocked in your community and beyond.

Then I want you to picture walking out to your car and getting in.

3 A portion of this section was originally published in my "Envision the End of Your Sin," *The Gospel Coalition* website, August 7, 2017, www.thegospelcoalition.org/article/envision -the-end-of-your-sin/.

Drive down the road near your house and circle your neighborhood a few times. Picture the place where you walked the dog with your children in the evenings.

Now, pull into your driveway and walk up to the door of your home.

Hear the scampering feet of your children running up to you and putting their arms around your legs, saying, "Daddy's home!" See the way they love and trust you.

Drink that in deeply.

Now, tell them to go outside and play because you must talk to Mommy about something. As you walk to the kitchen where she's faithfully going about her day, look at those smiling pictures on the wall. Remember the happy days you shared together.

Lead her by the hand to your bedroom where you used to make love.

Ask her to have a seat.

Feel your heart scamper and the lump form in your throat.

See her eyes ask what's wrong. Then watch her weep as you tell her you've been unfaithful.

Hear her wail.

See her sob.

Feel her hit your chest and watch her fall to her knees in despair.

Imagine the phone call to her parents, and to yours. Hear the silence on the phone as they take in what you've told them.

Imagine the day you gather your children and sit them down to explain why Mommy and Daddy are going to spend some time apart and sell the house they love so much.

See yourself taking down those smiling pictures from the wall and taping up the moving boxes, unsure if you'll ever open them again.

Do you see it?

Sin doesn't tell you about those days, does it?

Satan doesn't tell you sin's true cost, because the cost is too high. Plead with God to help you see the end of your sin. Also ask him to help you see that your sin doesn't just destroy your body, soul, and life, but others' as well.

Relational Fallout

Tim and Jess were certain they'd get married. They met online and quickly began spending time together. Laughter and conversation came easily, as did their physical attraction. Short kisses quickly gave way to making out. Within a few months, no boundary was uncrossed.

They professed love, but sex outside of marriage is not an act of true love. True love never does anything to harm another person's relationship with God. Love leads people toward Jesus, not away from him.

By giving into their sinful desires, Tim and Jess had begun to both defraud each other and lead each other toward divine judgment.[4]

Defrauding Others

When we sin sexually, we take something that is not ours. If you are unmarried, the person you engage in sexual activity with is *potentially someone else's spouse*. By sinning in this way, you are defrauding both that person and his or her future spouse. You are stealing something that isn't yours, because God hasn't given it to you.[5] Likewise, *you* are potentially someone else's spouse. By engaging in sexual activity, you are sinning against your future

---

4 1 Cor. 6:9; 1 Thess. 4:1–8; Heb. 13:4.
5 If you feel certain you're going to marry the person you're dating or engaged to, just remember that you don't know what tomorrow holds (James 4:13–17). I was engaged to a

spouse, even if you haven't met him or her yet, because you're giving away something God desires only your spouse to have.

This is especially serious for followers of Jesus. Christians show love through sexual purity. First Thessalonians 4:3–8 holds a wealth of truth, but let's focus on one idea:

> This is the will of God, your sanctification: that you abstain from sexual immorality. . . . No one [should] transgress and wrong his brother in this matter, because the Lord is an avenger in all these things. . . . For God has not called us for impurity, but in holiness. Therefore whoever disregards this, disregards not man but God, who gives his Holy Spirit to you.

Paul is making the relational significance of sexual sin especially clear. It *wrongs* our brothers and sisters in Christ. To "transgress" means to go beyond or step over the boundary God has given. Sexual sin transgresses the property of a brother or sister. The word *wrong* can be translated "defraud, take advantage of, gain something wrongfully." It describes selfish gain at the expense of another person. When we step over God's command to abstain from sexual immorality, our "gain" always comes at the expense of another person. Even if the sex is consensual, it is rooted in selfishness that places our wants above God's will (1 Thess. 4:3).[6]

---

different woman before I married my wife. We called off our wedding fifty days before it was to happen.

6 If you've been the victim of sexual experiences that were not consensual, I assure you that God sees and knows the evil that has happened to you. He promises justice against those who have harmed you and will bring healing to you as you lean upon his grace. Please do not keep your suffering in secret; invite a godly friend to help you speak to your pastor and seek professional help.

Love is not love. *God* is love, and any "love" that goes against his character or commands is a deadly imposter that steals life rather than gives it. Some view this as unloving and dangerously restrictive. They feel they have the right to define love and sex, but God alone has this right. And he calls the church to be a people set apart in purity so they can shine forth a reflection of his love to a watching world.

Degrading Others

The ultimate reason we shouldn't sin with someone sexually is not because he or she may one day be a spouse, but because he or she is already an image bearer. When sex is removed from the sacred space of marriage, it has a degrading effect on people made in God's image. This is evident in heart-wrenching evils like rape, sexual abuse, sex trafficking, prostitution, and adultery. But it's also true of what some consider harmless sins. Pornography, for example, has become so commonplace that many struggle to see its danger. Yet whether it's a popular TV series or a hardcore website, porn reduces the people being watched to mere servants of lust. They entertain; we indulge. We don't care about their names or their pains, only that they gratify our lust.

We forget that God created the men and women employed by the porn industry. They bear his image. They have souls. They are someone's son or daughter. They will spend eternity enjoying God's presence or suffering in misery under his wrath.[7] They cry real tears, feel real pain, experience real regrets. They have real stories, many of which are tragic accounts of abuse, desperation, and prostitution as their only option for survival. But porn entices you to forget their humanity and grieve their Maker.

---

7 Dan. 12:2; Matt. 25:46; John 5:29; Acts 24:15.

The effects of pornography don't stop there. It shapes the way we view and treat the people around us. Just recently, I was walking with a young man who'd been looking at porn daily for months. When we passed an attractive woman, he had a physical reaction in which he spun his head the other way and began to walk sideways with his back toward her. While I appreciated his desire not to lust, that is not the kind of response men should have toward women.

What we value in a potential spouse can be so corrupted by porn or sexual flings that no one seems interesting to us. We grow distrustful of fellow church members, seeing men as predators and women as temptresses.[8] Couples pursuing marriage can have their mutual trust crippled by sexual compromise.[9] Husbands and wives can develop unrealistic—and often dishonoring—"sexpectations," which can lead to pressuring one's spouse to engage in sexual acts he or she is uncomfortable with. Or they can fantasize about other lovers and use a spouse's body as a "mannequin for masturbation."[10] Satan comes to steal, kill, and destroy—and degrading sex is one of his favorite weapons.

Destroying Others

Christians are meant to help others see God more clearly through our lives and influence. We are to help each other fight sin's deceitfulness and fan the flame of persevering faith (Heb. 3:12–13). In sexual sin, we do the exact opposite. Our sin leads others to sin against God. Consider Jesus's sobering words:

---

8   See Jason Seville, "Corporate Consequences of Unchecked Porn Use," 9Marks website, October 30, 2018, www.9marks.org/article/corporate-consequences-of-unchecked-porn-use/.

9   See my "How to Destroy Your Marriage before It Begins," The Gospel Coalition website, September 11, 2013, www.thegospelcoalition.org/article/destroy-marriage-begins/.

10 Phrase taken from John Piper, *The Marks of a Spiritual Leader* (Minneapolis, MN: Desiring God, 2011), 45.

Whoever causes one of these little ones who believe in me to sin, it would be better for him to have a great millstone fastened around his neck and to be drowned in the depth of the sea. Woe to the world for temptations to sin! For it is necessary that temptations come, but woe to the one by whom the temptation comes. (Matt. 18:6–7)

Do you realize, friend, that when we commit sexual sin with others, we cause them to sin against God? We help them break fellowship and grieve his Spirit. We numb their affections and mute their prayers. We distract them from pursuing God's kingdom and righteousness. We burden their consciences and callous their hearts, setting them up for future temptations. We cause them to doubt God's goodness, dismiss his warnings, presume upon his mercy, challenge his authority, and provoke his jealousy.

Your sin, especially sexual sin, never affects just you—it always affects others. I shudder to think how many professing Christian men and women have embraced adultery—and had the audacity to blame God. "He just wants me to be happy." "This new relationship blesses me unlike any other."

How many single believers start dating unbelievers in their exasperation with waiting? They may explain their hopes of helping the person to see Jesus, or insist this is the only door God opened for them. More often than not, though, the compromises of "missionary dating" lead to hypocrisy and a confusing witness to both unbeliever and watching world.[11]

How many believers, dating or engaged, similarly compromise on clear boundaries in their infatuation? Overreacting to fears of

---

11 Missionary dating is dating someone who isn't a believer in Jesus yet, hoping he or she will become a Christian.

legalism can lead to foolishly avoiding clear boundaries. Affirmation or affection or gratification must never eclipse the responsibility we have to help one another see God with a pure heart.

Are you tempting someone else to sin against God? Is there someone who tempts you in this way, even if that person says he or she loves you? How should Jesus's warnings cause you to respond?

Salvation from the Fallout

Sin's fallout has left us all sexually broken. Some desire sex too much, while others desire sex with their spouse too little. Guilt and shame have left some of us feeling distant from God and unworthy of spousal love. Others of us have ruined relationships with people we deeply cared about, because we gave in to temptation. Biological challenges have left some of us in despair, while abuse has convinced others of us that sex is anything but beautiful.

On my wedding night, my wife ministered to me in my brokenness. She reminded me of the grace of Jesus and assured me that if God could forgive her, she was willing and desirous to forgive me. She led me to the bottomless well of grace and helped me drink afresh of the water Jesus promised for sinners like me (John 4:13–14).

No matter what form your sexual brokenness takes, Jesus came to save you from it. "Come to me," he invites, "all who labor and are heavy laden, and I will give you rest" (Matt. 11:28). No matter where you have been, what you have done, or what has been done to you, the grace of God can wash you clean, consecrate you as his child, and restore what sin has stolen.[12] For "where sin increased, grace abounded all the more" (Rom. 5:20).

---

12 In Joel 2:25, the Lord assures Israel, "I will restore to you the years / that the swarming locust has eaten." In response to Israel's sin, locusts had been sent to destroy its bountiful blessings, but God sends this promise to assure them that he will heal what sin had decimated.

Does your sin condemn you? "There is therefore now no condemnation for those who are in Christ Jesus" (Rom. 8:1). Consider what he has saved us from:

> Do you not know that the unrighteous will not inherit the kingdom of God? Do not be deceived: neither the sexually immoral, nor idolaters, nor adulterers, nor men who practice homosexuality, nor thieves, nor the greedy, nor drunkards, nor revilers, nor swindlers will inherit the kingdom of God. And such were some of you. But you were washed, you were sanctified, you were justified in the name of the Lord Jesus Christ and by the Spirit of our God. (1 Cor. 6:9–11)

Are you dirty? Grace washes clean. Are you shameful? Grace sets you apart with honor. Are you guilty? Grace makes you stand forgiven.

Jesus also came to liberate us from sin's consequences (Gal. 1:4). In crucifixion he took our guilt, and through resurrection he overcame the curse. By faith we are united with him, which means salvation is deliverance not only from sin's condemnation, but also from its consequences. God's Spirit liberates us from sin and empowers obedience to Jesus. We now "walk in newness of life" (Rom. 6:4), the gift of saving grace. As we journey toward glory, we do so with our eyes fixed on Jesus, who calls us to confidently "draw near to the throne of grace . . . [to] receive mercy and find grace to help in [your] time of need" (Heb. 4:16).

The rest of this book is devoted to helping you practically pursue the purity of heart that allows you to see this God of grace.

PART 2

———

PATHWAYS TO PURITY

ONE COOL TEXAS AFTERNOON, the late Howard Hendricks took a walk with a young seminary student. "Prof" was in his eighties, and he wore a sunken skull and eye patch as badges of victory over a battle with cancer. His body had faded, but his holiness and wisdom had not.

As they talked, the young man asked the aged saint, "When will I ever be free from my battle with lust?" After a moment of silence, Prof slowed his stroll and put his arm around the man's shoulder. With a wearied grin he said, "I don't know, young man. I haven't gotten there yet. But we're getting closer."

The pursuit of purity is a lifelong battle. It will endure until the great day when sin will be no more. This reminder is important because as we move into the pathways section of this book, we must have reasonable expectations.

What I am about to share are not quick fixes. There are no magic pills to make you pure. There is no hidden verse that will forever do away with the struggle.

This is about the long haul. Some of you are getting kicked in the face today, which makes seeing clearly very difficult.

What follows is about learning *how* to take the next step on the path of purity.

It's about learning to lean inward and look upward, with the hopes of seeing Jesus just a little clearer each day.

It is about helping you avoid today's temptation to escape loneliness through sin.

It is about laboring toward less regret in the months and years ahead.

It is about walking down the aisle more pure than you otherwise would have.

It is about saving your marriage twenty years down the road.

It is about looking at your spouse on his or her deathbed and saying, "We made it."

It is about remaining faithful in your singleness until the day Jesus takes you home.

It is about hearing "Well done, good and faithful servant" on that last day.

These are long-term strategies to help you pursue the promise "Blessed are the pure in heart, for they shall see God."

Let's get started.

6

Feed Your Heart

HARRY MENDENHALL WAS AN ATTORNEY for an international shipping company in Portland, Oregon. His luxurious lifestyle afforded travel to exotic places and the ability to enjoy any pleasure he desired. Mendenhall thought he had it all—until he and his wife read the Gospel of John. They heard of promised water that would quench their thirst, and heavenly bread that would satisfy their hunger. As they beheld Jesus, God transformed their hearts and they were born again.

A few weeks after their conversion, their pastor preached from 2 Corinthians 5:17: "If anyone is in Christ, he is a new creation. The old has passed away; behold, the new has come!" Afterward Harry approached the pastor: "I liked your sermon, but it was deficient. Can you come to dinner so I can explain?" Their pastor humbly accepted the invitation and set a date to meet Harry in his home.

The Mendenhall home rested on a bluff overlooking the Willamette River. The pastor made his way to the front door, where Harry welcomed him. They made their way to a window overlooking the garden, where Harry described the beauty of a flowering bush. They walked to another window, where Harry described a large tree in the yard. As Harry led his pastor to window after window, he pointed to various objects of creation and detailed what he saw.

Finally, Harry explained: "Your sermon was lovely and helped me greatly, but you left out one thing when you said all things were new—you never mentioned new eyes! I got new eyes when I came to Christ. For fifty years I lived for two things: money and sex. And that's all I ever saw. I never saw a sunset. I never saw a flower. I never saw a tree. I never even saw the river! But now, I've got new eyes, and everything is new."[1]

When we come to Christ, the Spirit makes us alive and gives us a new heart and new eyes. We begin to see glories we never saw before. Our new heart has new loves, new hates, and new desires. In a sense, we get a taste of what Adam and Eve threw away when they traded God for a piece of fruit.

Come and Enjoy God

God created Eden as a playground of pleasure. The air exuded nectar, trees displayed brilliant leaves, fruits dangled on every limb. It was a world of wonder that brought delight to God and his people.[2] Into this garden, God placed our first parents. He wired them for pleasure by giving them ears to snatch sounds, noses to catch smells, tongues to enjoy tastes, and eyes to behold God and his beautiful creation.

1 This story comes from the wonderful sermon series on regeneration by Richard Owen Roberts. This quote is from "Regeneration in Connection with Backsliding, Evangelism, Effectual Calling: A New Creation," International Awakening Ministries, CD-ROM.

2 The Hebrew word that we translate as "Eden" is associated with words that mean delight, pleasure, enjoyment, pleasantness (see Ps. 36:8, "river of your delights").

Readied for pleasure, Adam was invited to indulge: "You may surely eat of every tree of the garden" (Gen. 2:16–17). It's as if God said, "Look! I made it all for you to enjoy. Take and eat." Even God's warning about the forbidden fruit was designed to protect their joy. *Do you think of God as a pleasure giver?*

When Satan infiltrated Eden, however, he came with a vengeance. The tempter persuaded Eve to believe that God was holding out on them, that the forbidden tree would make them happy.[3] *How could something so lovely be bad?*

Adam and Eve believed his lie, and when they ate, they died, just as God warned. A shadow of death descended on the land of delight. Spiritual darkness choked out the garden's glory and dimmed its residents' eyes. No longer could they see the beauty of God or the radiance of their surrounding world. Impending physical death was eclipsed by an even worse tragedy: spiritual death. Sin had promised life, yet it robbed and left them bound in sorrow and shame.

Our exit from Eden has thrown us into a world of confusion. Though God's likeness in us remains, it is marred. We're still drawn to beauty and pleasure, but not always as we should be. Our sinful flesh highjacks right desires and directs them toward wrong ends.

Change Your Diet

Jessie's walk with God slowed almost as soon as she started college. Parties replaced church. Scripture remained shut. Prayers were

---

3 It is interesting that Satan's temptation to Adam and Eve was to become like God in the sense that they would know the difference between "good and evil" (Gen. 2:17). Satan's ploy was to present what God says is bad as actually being a good thing, while assuring them that God is withholding good from them. But God's command was given to keep them from pain, not pleasure.

hurried or absent. Social life, social media, and occasional bouts with porn consumed her downtime. She still believed, but years of apathy had sapped her affections for God. She wanted to change, but had no clue how.

She needed to change her diet, my wife and I explained, which would change her appetite. She needed to fast from what sapped her love for God and feast upon what stirred it. We assured her that, over time, hunger for Christ would increase and prevail over taste for sin.

In Galatians 6, we are warned: "Do not be deceived: God is not mocked, for whatever one sows, that will he also reap. For the one who sows to his own flesh will from the flesh reap corruption, but the one who sows to the Spirit will from the Spirit reap eternal life" (Gal. 6:7–8). What you sow determines what you reap. What you feast on affects what you love.

We asked Jessie to write down how she used her time through-out the next week. The discovery startled her: she rarely thought of God. At times she sensed his Spirit inviting her to commune with Jesus, but almost always she turned to her phone, friends, or other pressing tasks. She had resisted him so many times that she now rarely heard his voice. No wonder her affections for him were weak.

Our affections are stirred toward what we feed them. You cannot stir eternal affections by sowing to earthly escapes. What happens to your affections if you fill your spare moments soaking in cable news and social media? Wherever you retreat for refreshment will form your affections.

"Blessed are those who hunger and thirst for righteousness," Jesus promises, "for they shall be satisfied" (Matt. 5:6). Feasting on him through faith will satisfy us—but sin would have us do anything but that. Sin saps our appetite for God; it's like consuming a bag of cotton candy before sitting down to a lavish dinner. Your desire for the feast is gone because you consumed a lesser delight.

Even things that aren't sinful can erode heavenly-mindedness (1 Cor. 10:23). Certainly, things like social media, novels, academics, athletics, movies, vacations, remodeling projects, and so on are not necessarily sinful. But as you consider them, do not ask, *How much of this can I enjoy before it becomes sin?* but rather, *Does this stir or sap my affections for Jesus?*

Just as in Eden, God has set before us a banquet of grace to feast on:

> Come, everyone who thirsts,
>   come to the waters;
> and he who has no money,
>   come, buy and eat!
> Come, buy wine and milk
>   without money and without price.
> Why do you spend your money for that which is not bread,
>   and your labor for that which does not satisfy?
> Listen diligently to me, and eat what is good,
>   and delight yourselves in rich food. (Isa. 55:1–2)

By feasting on provisions of grace, God deepens our affections for him and weakens our affections for sin.

Feed Your Affections

What follows are scriptural prescriptions to warm your affections. These are not God's only provisions, but they are his surest fountains of mercy. It is as if he has pointed to them and said; "Come!

You can always find me here."[4] As you consider them, keep two things in mind.

1. Feast by Faith, Not Feeling. At times your desires for God will be ablaze, but most often you won't *feel* his presence. God often withholds feelings of his presence in order to strengthen our faith (2 Cor. 5:7). Faith and feeling are not opposed to each other; both are ours in Christ. But faith informed by God's word must always guide our feelings, not the other way around.

2. Pursue Intimacy with God. Jumping through religious hoops will not warm your heart toward God. "You will seek me and find me," he promises, "when you seek me with all your heart" (Jer. 29:13).

Obeying the charge to "train yourself for godliness" is not legalism (1 Tim. 4:7–8).[5] Just as it isn't legalistic to say, "Keep breathing air and eating food," it isn't legalistic to strive to know and obey God. Striving for holiness is not legalism; it's worship.

Scripture: Feast on God's Word

Jesus insists, "Man shall not live by bread alone, but by every word that comes from the mouth of God" (Matt. 4:4, quoting Deut. 8:3). As bodies cannot survive apart from food, so our souls will starve if we neglect God's word. Scripture invites us to a banquet through which we taste and see that he is good (Ps. 34:8; 1 Pet. 2:2–3).

"How can a young man keep his way pure?" the psalmist asked. "By guarding it according to your word" (Ps. 119:9). God's word keeps us on the path of purity because it changes what we love. We

---

4 These disciplines are lived out individually and corporately. Chapter 7 is dedicated entirely to how we live out our devotion to Christ in the context of community.

5 By legalism, I mean empty, dead religion that is focused on exterior actions and is void of internal affections driven by faith and delight in God.

will love the wrong things if our minds aren't filled with God's truth. Your sin and your Bible cannot mix for long: either the Scriptures will keep you from sin, or sin will keep you from the Scriptures.[6]

Listening to God produces love for God. This is why we must regularly step away, turn off our devices, and seek his voice. Come to your Bible as a beggar looking for bread. Note passages that move you. Mark them in your Bible. Meditate on them. Memorize them. Store up spiritual truths in your heart so that when you're in the heat of battle and not thinking clearly, you have an armory of verses you can grab like a fire extinguisher to put out temptation's flames.[7]

Along with personal study, God's people regularly gather to hear Scripture proclaimed.[8] Don't settle for weak preaching consisting of a few verses, some cute stories, and a couple laughs. That sort of preaching will not help you fight sin. Join a church that preaches the glory of Jesus—and feast on it every week. Build word-saturated relationships in that fellowship.

Feasting on Scripture brings you face-to-face with the author and provides power for the fight. Open your Bible and watch his holiness humble you, his wisdom comfort you, his beauty captivate you, and his love astound you.

Why do we begin with God's word? Because it teaches us how to pursue all the other means of grace.

Prayer and Fasting: Delight in God

"Watch and pray that you may not fall into temptation," Jesus warned his disciples (Matt. 26:41). It is very difficult to look at porn

---

6 This quote has been attributed in various forms to J. C. Ryle and D. L. Moody.

7 Passages I go back to regularly in times of battle are Ps. 16:11; Matt. 5:6, 8; Rom. 6:1–13; 1 Cor. 10:13; Heb. 2:18; 4:14–16; 12:14; Rev. 20:11–15; 21–22.

8 See Heb. 10:24–25; 1 Tim. 4:13; 2 Tim. 4:2; 1 Cor. 14:23–25.

if you are on your face in prayer. When temptation calls, your first response should be to cry to God for help. And pray expectantly, like the psalmist:

> My soul waits for the LORD
>   more than watchmen for the morning,
>   more than watchmen for the morning. (Ps. 130:6)

But we shouldn't pray only during attack, of course. Prayer is like breathing for the Christian; if we neglect it, our soul will shrivel. So just as you breathe continually, pray continually (1 Thess. 5:17).

Pray God's word. God promises that if we pray according to his will, he will answer (1 John 5:14). So echo Moses's prayer to see God's glory, asking him to fulfill his eternal purpose of making you like Jesus (Ex. 33:18; Rom. 8:29). Pray for a heart that hates sin and hungers for holiness.[9] God loves to answer prayer according to his promises, so fill your prayers with his word.

Pray for protection. The psalmist pleaded, "Keep back your servant from presumptuous sins; / let them not have dominion over me!" (Ps. 19:13). Likewise, Jesus taught his disciples to pray, "Lead us not into temptation, but deliver us from evil" (Matt. 6:13). We pray for protection from the tempter with rock-solid assurance: "He who is in you is greater than he who is in the world" (1 John 4:4).

Pray with perseverance. Jesus said, "Ask, and it will be given to you; seek, and you will find; knock, and it will be opened to you." This isn't a call to pray once and quit, but to continually cry out

---

9 Consider these passages to fuel your prayers: Pss. 34:14; 51:10; 97:10; Prov. 8:13; Amos 5:15; Rom.12:9; Heb. 12:14; 1 Pet. 3:10–11.

to God.[10] You cannot microwave holiness. It must be fought for. By persevering in prayer, your gaze will be fixed on Christ, which God will use to transform you (2 Cor. 3:18).[11]

So, do you pray? Do you daily retreat from everything to speak with God (Matt. 6:6)? Do you have a spirit of prayer throughout the day in which you converse with him in all you do? Prayerfulness yields nearness to God and likeness to him that we must have to inherit salvation (John 15:1–6; Heb. 12:14).

Do you fast? Prayerful fasting is one of the most potent weapons in fighting sexual sin. Sin is all about self-indulgence; fasting is a way to punch indulgence in the throat. When we fast, we say no to something in order to say yes to focused time with God. By telling our body *no* to something it's craving (food, entertainment, etc.), we're reawakened to the fact that we're dependent creatures. And this gives us opportunity to cry out, *As my body hungers for food, make my soul hunger for you.*[12]

Like all disciplines, mere fasting will not fill you with the joy of Jesus. In fact, God often uses fasting to expose our grumpiness about our discomfort. But when we fast in faith, God starves our sin and focuses our sight on him. Jesus *assumes* his disciples will fast as they await their bridegroom's return (Matt. 6:16–18; 9:14–15), so ask another brother or sister to join with you and seek God together.[13]

10 The verbs *ask*, *seek*, and *knock* in Matthew 7:7 are in the present active imperative form. *Present* means it's to be an ongoing act. *Active* means it's something we do. And *imperative* means it's a command. A faithful translation could read, "Keep on asking, keep on seeking, keep on knocking."
11 See chapter 2 for a fuller explanation.
12 Apart from the Bible, the most impactful resource I have found on prayer is the short book *A Call to Prayer* by J. C. Ryle. I highly commend it.
13 One form of fasting is observing the Sabbath. Though Jesus has fulfilled the law's requirements of the Sabbath, it is wise to regularly retreat and rest in God.

Ordinances: Remember Jesus Together

When the church gathers, it should pray, sing, proclaim God's word, and remember Jesus through baptism and the Lord's Supper. Jesus gave us these ordinances so that together we might freshly consider his saving and sustaining mercies.[14]

Through baptism, we hear testimony of God's grace and see a picture of his power to raise people from the dead. In the Lord's Supper, we see symbols of bread and wine, which aid us in remembering Jesus's body and blood. As we partake of them in faith, the Spirit strengthens our communion with Jesus and deepens our love for other believers.[15]

God has not given these ordinances as empty rituals, but as unifying and purifying graces.[16] Baptism and the Lord's Supper point us to the Savior who died and rose to free us from sin. Remembering him in this way produces humble contrition and hopeful celebration that transforms us into his likeness.

Music: Stir Your Soul with Singing

God loves music. The Bible's longest book is a hymnbook.[17] Heaven will forever be filled with singing. God himself will sing over us.[18] In the meantime, singing his truth is a weapon that feeds affections

14 An "ordinance" is something that is ordained or commanded by someone in authority—in this case, God. A "sacrament" is something that is sacred, or set apart by God with special meaning. Either word can be used, but I prefer "ordinance" because it avoids confusion that these elements could have any kind of saving power.

15 First Corinthians 10:16 speaks of our "participation" with Christ through taking the Lord's Supper. This highlights a unique means of grace God gives as we remember Jesus's death.

16 God gives severe warnings in 1 Corinthians 11:27–30 about believers taking the Supper in an "unworthy manner." To turn God's gracious gift into an empty ritual in which you partake without pursuing forgiveness with others, or repentance for your own sin, is perilous for your soul.

17 The book of Psalms.

18 Zeph. 3:17; Rev. 5:8–11; 14:1–5.

and fights temptation. Martin Luther even claimed that Satan "flees before the sound of music almost as he takes flight at the word of theology."[19]

While not everyone resonates with music in the same way, God uses it to inform our minds and warm our souls. Tune-wrapped truths have a way of stirring us to delight in God. If we sing songs about lovers, we should certainly sing to the God of love.

Study the great hymns and songs of the faith. Find lyrics that help you look to God. For instance, my soul is served when I sing:

> Prone to wander, Lord, I feel it,
> Prone to leave the God I love;
> Here's my heart, O take and seal it;
> Seal it for thy courts above.[20]

I hate how my heart is so easily tempted to sin; that song gives me a way to plead for God to change me.

Make a playlist of songs you can turn on when you're feeling tempted. Temptation disorients, but uplifting lyrics of truth can drown out sin's voice and point your soul toward its only satisfaction.

Creation: Amazed by His Wisdom

Nature may be one of God's most surprising weapons against lust. Whether we peer through a telescope or microscope, the created order gives manifold witness to the beauty and creativity

---

19 Martin Luther, *Letters II*, vol. 49 of *Luther's Works*, American Edition, ed. Jaroslav Pelikan, Hilton C. Oswald, and Helmut T. Lehmann (Philadelphia: Fortress, 1999), 426–29.

20 "Come, Thou Fount of Every Blessing," Robert Robinson, 1758, hymnary.org/text/come_thou_fount_of_every_blessing/.

of God.[21] God's fingerprints are everywhere, and they help us kill sin.[22]

Humans are curious creatures. From childhood, discovering exciting new things thrills us. But sin preys on our curiosity by stirring our flesh to explore evil. It whispers to our heart, *Where will this link lead me?* or *What might it be like to be with that person?* Instead of feeding sinful curiosity, take walks, watch sunsets, and listen to birds sing. As you do, praise God for his creativity and ask him to awaken your affections for his beauty alone.[23] Sin flourishes in fantasy, but God can use even the smell of honeysuckle or the grandeur of a sunset to tether us to reality.[24]

Heaven: We Will See His Face

When Christ returns, we will regain all that was lost in Eden. Sin will be banished, affliction healed, shame silenced, and tears forever wiped away. Yet the greatest wonder of heaven is that we will no longer know God by faith. In that land, we shall "be like him" and "see his face" (Phil. 3:21; 1 John 3:2; Rev. 22:4). When the hope of seeing God fills our hearts, it has a purifying effect on our lives.[25]

21 See "Great Is Thy Faithfulness," Thomas Chisholm, 1923, hymnary.org/text/great_is_thy_faithfulness_o_god_my_fathe/.

22 Psalm 104 takes us on a tour of God's creation, recounting the wonder of his benevolence. The psalm concludes with praise to the almighty architect—and assures us that not doing so is foolishness that leads to judgment (see Rom. 1:18–32).

23 See John Piper, "The Pleasure of God in His Creation," Desiring God website, February 8, 1987, www.desiringgod.org/messages/the-pleasure-of-god-in-his-creation.

24 Many faithful pastors have given creation as a prescription for fighting sin and the sadness that accompanies it. See, for example, Jonathan Edwards, *The Works of Jonathan Edwards*, vol. 13, no. 108, The *"Miscellanies": Entry nos. a–z, aa–zz, 1–500*, ed. Thomas A. Schafer (New Haven, CT: Yale University Press, 1994); Charles Spurgeon, "The Minister's Fainting Fits" (Peabody, MA: Hendrickson, 2010), 163–64; and John Piper, *The Pleasures of God* (Sisters, OR: Multnomah, 1991), chap. 3.

25 To further study this fascinating theme, see Matt. 5:8; 24:42–46; Rom. 13:11–14; 1 Cor. 15:58; 2 Cor. 7:1; Col. 3:1–5; 1 Thess. 3:13; 5:23; 1 Pet. 1:13; 2 Peter 3:14; 1 John 2:28–3:3.

On the last day, we will stand in God's light, and all our deeds will be exposed.[26] When you are tempted today, remember the last day.

Struggling saint, as your flesh pulls you downward, set your mind on Christ above (Col. 3:1–4). When sin promises escape, envision the day of judgment. When temptation beckons, consider that God is watching your response. Make decisions today that you will be grateful for ten thousand years from now. With each passing moment, we draw nearer to that day when we'll be saved to sin no more.[27] Until then, read often of heaven and ask God to make you homesick for that everlasting city where the pure in heart will see him at last.[28]

God is gracious to supply strength without our asking, but we ought never to presume upon his grace. The Scriptures call us to cultivate our affections through faith-filled discipline. And the Spirit uses these means of grace to awaken our affections, so that our hearts cry out with David,

> One thing have I asked of the LORD,
>   that will I seek after:
> that I may dwell in the house of the LORD
>   all the days of my life,
> to gaze upon the beauty of the LORD. (Ps. 27:4)

---

26 1 Cor. 4:5; 2 Cor. 5:9–10; Rev. 20:11–15.
27 "There Is a Fountain," William Cowper and Lowell Mason, 1772, hymnary.org/text/there_is_a_fountain_filled_with_blood_dr/.
28 See Isa. 65:17; 66:22; 2 Pet. 3:13; Rev. 21–22.

7

Help Others Home

THE BATTLE AT KRUGER took place near a watering hole in Kruger National Park, South Africa. As a herd of Cape buffalo approached the shore, they came upon several lions crouching along the path. When the first buffalo saw the lions, it turned to flee.

The lionesses pursued and pounced on a straggling calf, barrel-rolling it down the bank and into the water. As they dragged the calf onto shore, a crocodile sprung from the shallows and latched onto the calf. A tug-of-war ensued, until the lions prevailed and lay down to feast.

While hope seemed lost for the calf, the entire herd of buffalo began running toward their fallen friend. They surrounded the lions and began to charge them. One lion was chased off while another was tossed through the air by a bull's horns. One by one, the lions were stomped, gored, and shooed away.

A bystander murmured, "It's too late." But another exclaimed, "Wait! Look! He's still alive. He's standing up. They've got him back!" And sure enough, somehow, the feeble and bloodied calf rose to its feet and scampered into the safety of the herd. The calf lived to see another day.

In many ways, that herd captures what God intends a local church to be.[1] On the outside the enemy prowls and seeks to devour, like the lions in our story (see Gen. 4:7; 1 Pet. 5:8). Sin isolates us from others and begins to consume. The church, however, resolves to love and do whatever it takes to help each other cling to Jesus and persevere to heaven.

The church is a primary means God uses to help you persevere in faith and be conformed to Jesus. You will not grow in purity or maturity apart from gospel community. Yes, there are exceptions to the rule, but pride tempts us to excuse isolation, to our detriment.

Help toward Heaven

God gives the church to help you resist temptation and draw you in a better direction, toward a better country. Our journey of faith is marked by the joyful assurance that God is with us and that soon we shall be with him.

But this journey cannot be made alone; we make it together. You need other Christians, and they need you. The remainder of this chapter considers how God wants to use the fellowship of a church to help you fight sexual sin and endure in faith.

Commit to One Another

When God calls you to himself, he calls you into the church. Our union with Jesus necessarily unites us with other believers. A healthy congregation faithfully preaches Christ *and* fervently helps its

---

1 Throughout this chapter, *church* refers to a local, geographically based gathering of believers. While we are united with the universal church (all believers everywhere), the New Testament focuses on how believers live out their faith with each other in local churches.

HELP OTHERS HOME

members live for him. The deep fellowship and soul-strengthening friendships we need to fight for purity are best formed in our local church community.[2]

Commitment to a church is not optional for a believer; it is commanded.[3] The commands to "exhort one another every day" and "not neglecting to meet together" *assume* we're intentionally gathering (Heb. 3:13; 10:24–25; 13:17). They assume we're actively involved in regular conversation about our spiritual condition. Let me put it this way: from the perspective of Scripture, it should be abnormal for a Christian to go a single week without a soul-strengthening, sin-fighting, Christ-honoring conversation with another believer.[4] We are created to know and be known by each other.

It has been said that it takes a village to raise a child. I say it takes a church to raise a Christian. For many years I attended church but remained in isolation. I showed up, worshiped, and even ministered, but I didn't experience the kind of persistent love that marks a New Testament church. It was mainly my fault, of course, and the effects were devastating. No one knew the state of my soul, or how it was being choked by hidden sin.

Again, sin thrives in the dark but withers in the light. That is, it withers when brought into the open of godly community. Selfishness, busy schedules, and spiritual laziness are enemies of the love that help us follow Jesus.

You cannot help everyone in your church in the same way, but you can commit to a few close friends. Though I am generally

---

2 Matt. 28:16–20; Acts 2:38–47; Eph. 2:11–22; 1 John 1:3.

3 It is impossible to obey the "one another" commands of the New Testament without commitment to a local community of believers who know, love, and care for each other.

4 Ephesians 4:25–32 (among other scriptures) specifically portrays the Christian life as being deeply intertwined in relationships that fight off sin while pursuing Christlike purity.

opposed to group texts, I have ongoing text conversations with two groups of brothers who exhort and pray for one another in the area of sexual purity. We confess our temptations, share God's word, and celebrate his goodness.

These brothers always know my "spiritual pulse." Meaning, if you called any of them right now, they could tell you accurately how my soul is and what my temptations are in this season. This is a live conversation for us because sin is still alive and crouching along our path.

A healthy church helps married couples fight sin together, and it also cultivates the community that single people need to fight for holiness. When God said, "It is not good that the man should be alone" (Gen. 2:18), he was highlighting our need for intimate community, not just the gift of marriage. In the church, single and married folk share time, tears, laughs, meals, and innumerable life experiences. While many may long for marriage, God gives tangible love through his people in a way that fleeting lust simply cannot compare.

To my single brothers and sisters who long to be married, I recognize it can be maddening to fight back relational and sexual urges that are so natural. At times you may feel as if God is withholding something very good from you, for reasons you can't understand. Please do not lose sight of the fact that God has not forgotten you. The fellowship of his people is a gift to help you combat loneliness. While it's true that fellowship doesn't quench sexual urges, God's physical provision of love through his people supplies tangible mercy that he uses to bring joy, comfort, and encouragement as you resist temptation. If you are feeling isolated, prayerfully reach out to your pastors and help them better serve the members of your church in this area.

Who are you helping to follow Jesus today? What keeps you from being helped in this way?

Warn One Another

The apostle James solemnly assured us, "My brothers, if anyone among you wanders from the truth and someone brings him back, let him know that whoever brings back a sinner from his wandering will save his soul from death and will cover a multitude of sins" (James 5:19–20).

Jesus left heaven to seek and save the lost, to pursue wayward sheep, and to show us the Father who runs to embrace prodigals (Luke 15:1–32; 19:10). The same sinner-seeking love that marked Jesus ought to mark his people. Yet Satan craftily schemes to keep us from caring for each other in this way. While he ensnares one, he deceitfully assures others to leave them alone, lest the friends appear nosy and judgmental.

But God's people mustn't stand by and watch one another be devoured by sin. Rather, we must "exhort one another every day, as long as it is called 'today,' that none of you may be hardened by the deceitfulness of sin" (Heb. 3:13). This verse assumes believers take sin's danger seriously, are actively discussing ways to fight it, and are continually hoping for the day when they will sin no more.

If someone does become ensnared, we imitate Jesus by going after him or her. The apostle Paul exhorts: "Brothers, if anyone is caught in any transgression, you who are spiritual should restore him in a spirit of gentleness" (Gal. 6:1). Our attempts at reproof and reconciliation should be marked by urgency and prayerfulness, not anger or exasperation. I'm reminded of a group of sisters from our church who learned that a fellow sister had become involved in a sexually immoral relationship. Rather than shun her, they prayed, fasted, and planned an intervention. At first the straying sister was angered, but as her friends tearfully explained their concern, her countenance changed and she agreed to let them help her repent (see Matt. 18:15–16).

If you were ensnared in sin, who would come to rescue you? Are you developing intentional, transparent, accountable relationships with other believers?

God gives real warnings to his people as a means of helping them persevere in faith. Hearing that "our God is a consuming fire" and that without holiness "no one will see the Lord" provokes a believer to cling to Jesus by faith.[5] The church is God's appointed means to ensure that the warnings in his word are regularly proclaimed.

We are not all weak in the same way, nor are we all strong at the same time. But together we remind each other of truth so that none of us is hardened by sin and hindered from heaven's calling. Don't allow fear to hinder you from loving others enough to warn them of the destruction that lurks on the road of rebellion.[6]

Rescue One Another

David came to the church alone that night. He grew up in church, but his attraction to men made him feel excluded, dirty, and shameful. A group claiming Christians can live a gay lifestyle and still please God had begun to woo him, but deep down he didn't trust

---

5   Hebrews contains five strong warnings against forsaking Christ (2:1–4; 3:7–4:13; 5:11–6:20; 10:19–39; and these quoted from 12:12–29). Similar warnings are echoed throughout the New Testament, including Matt. 5:13; 24:13; John 8:31; 15:6; Rom. 11:22; 1 Cor. 9:27; 10:12; 15:1; Col. 1:22–23; 1 Tim. 4:1; 2 Tim. 2:12; 1 John 2:19; 2 John 1:9; Jude 20–21; Rev. 2–3; 14:12; 21:7.

6   To hear how God's warnings rescued me, see my article "I Was a Pastor Hooked on Porn," The Gospel Coalition website, August 22, 2017, www.thegospelcoalition.org/article/i-was -pastor-hooked-on-porn/.

their message. That night he heard a friend of our church share about his own struggle with same-sex attraction and how the love of fellow Christians had been a refuge for him.[7]

David heard compassionate truth and met other believers who embodied it. And the Lord used that night to change the trajectory of his walk with God. Today he is a faithful member who, while still battling same-sex attraction, strives to honor God with the help of many brothers.

Christians are people who "speak the truth in love" with one another (Eph. 4:15). This means we love each other enough to be honest about our struggles, and we care enough to help others with theirs. We pursue each other and discuss uncomfortable areas of our sin, for we know isolation is the enemy of purity and darkness the breeding ground for sin.

But being "authentic" is not an end in itself. Satan is glad for people to talk openly about their sin—so long as they make no strides toward repentance. There is a hypocrisy that appears earnest—even shedding tears in confession—yet makes no real steps to change. We must develop healthy relationships that graciously push each other toward honesty and repentance.

Are you developing intentionally intrusive relationships in which you are giving and receiving godly encouragement, confession, and rebuke?

Sharing with those who have similar struggles can provide empathy and insight, but may also prove unhelpful at times. If your accountability partner is actively sinning in the same way you are, the temptation to be overly sympathetic and withhold strong words

---

7 You can listen to the same talk: Sam Allberry, "The Gospel and Same-Sex Attraction," April 22, 2016, delraybaptist.org/resources/seminars/the-gospel-and-same-sex-attraction/.

of warning can take over. Someone who knows his own need for grace, but who isn't entrenched in the same sin, may be freer to offer the words you need.

This is certainly (though not exclusively) important for believers who struggle with same-sex attraction. It's vital for such believers, like David, to develop healthy relationships with members of the same sex. Accountability relationships should be with someone of the same sex, but not with someone tempted toward same-sex attraction. Satan can prey upon a mutual struggle to disastrous ends.

Satan also undermines honest relationships through shame. Many women with strong sexual desires are hesitant to share because, as one sister said, "Everybody will think I'm a hoochie." Many feel shameful because the church has too often addressed lust, pornography, and masturbation only as temptations men struggle with. This perception is just not accurate. Candid conversations about sexuality among sisters may take extra work, but they must happen. The temptation to compare with others can be crushing. It will take courage to share, especially the first time, but God will supply it, as well as the ability to respond well. If you don't struggle in this area but a sister risks sharing with you, pursue her compassionately and consistently.

Though it's never safe to sin, a healthy church will be a safe place to struggle. We're not all sexually broken in the same way, but we all stand equally in need of grace. Learning to be vulnerable together can be scary.

And the fact is—other Christians will hurt you. We will misunderstand each other. There may be times we forget to check in when someone is hurting. We may act overbearing when we should back off. We may grow impatient toward someone genuinely trying. Pursuing holiness is messy. But God will use our failures and forgiveness alike to shape us into the image of his Son.

Struggle alongside One Another

Richard and Andy worked in a factory outside a West Texas town. Andy's new faith was growing, but he told Richard his drive home was a daily battle. A few miles from his house was a fork in the road: a left turn led home, but a right took him to the strip club that had long been his escape.

One afternoon, Andy confessed he craved to go to the club after work. Before Richard left, he prayed with Andy and assured him Jesus would help him resist.

It was pouring rain when Andy began his drive. Approaching the fork in the road, he noticed something in the median. As the windshield wipers brushed aside the rain, he saw Richard standing at the fork with a large piece of cardboard. On it was an arrow pointing home. Andy turned left toward home that day, and every day since.

Do you regularly talk about Jesus with fellow believers? Are you a sign-holder for struggling sheep?

Satan would have us do anything but remind each other of the inexhaustible riches we have in Jesus.

Jesus is God's final Word, the risen one who equips us to do what is pleasing in his sight. He sympathizes with our weaknesses and stands ready to bestow mercy in our time of need. Jesus is our sure and steady anchor who holds us firm in temptation's tossing seas (Heb. 6:19–20).

Jesus is our risen high priest who eternally lives to make intercession for us. His completed work secures our redemption and assures us God will remember our sins no more.[8] Jesus appears in God's

---

8 The theme of Jesus being seated is prominent in Hebrews (1:3; 8:1; 10:12; 12:2). There were no chairs in the Old Testament temple, because a priest's work was never done. Yet Jesus is seated in glory because his work has been completed—as he assures through his declaration from the cross, "It is finished!"

presence on our behalf, enabling us to hold fast to our confession with hope of promised reward.[9]

When feelings of discontentment tempt us toward sin, we point to Jesus who promises to never leave or forsake us (Heb. 13:5–6). Though our feelings, emotions, and physical stamina are ever changing, our hope rests in him who is the same yesterday, today, and forever (13:8).

As we encourage each other with these truths today, we keep an eye toward the eternal day in which we shall see him face to face. Hope for Jesus's return must remain in the forefront of our minds, hearts, and conversations.[10]

Even now, Jesus prepares to return for those eagerly awaiting him (Heb. 9:28; 10:13). So as we await that fast-approaching day, may we help each other toward heaven. May we *gather* weekly to fix our eyes on him through receiving his word, singing, praying, baptizing, and sharing in the Supper he gave. Then may we *scatter* to call the lost to believe, all the while helping each other obey his commands. May we do this day by day, until it is no longer called today.

Come soon, Lord Jesus. Come soon.

---

9 See Heb. 7:25; 8:12; 9:12, 24; 10:17, 23.
10 See Heb. 12:12; Isa. 40:1–2; Luke 21:28; 1 Thess. 4:18; 5:11–14.

8

Enter the Light

"I FEEL GROSS AND I DON'T KNOW what to do," Taylor said, staring at her coffee.

"I know it's hard to talk about," Jasmine replied, "but maybe start by telling me what happened."

Taylor looked at her phone and explained that she had stayed up talking to strangers online. After a few follow-up questions she admitted the conversations were sexual, she had masturbated, and she had almost sent pictures of herself.

Jasmine could tell it weighed heavily on Taylor, but she knew the Lord was the place to start: "Have you talked to God about it yet?"

Taylor seemed confused: "Not really. I mean, he already knows, right?"

"Sure, God knows, but you still need to seek his help," Jasmine explained. "He still loves you, and he wants you to talk to him about your sin."

Taylor admitted she rarely confessed sins to God. She usually felt guilty for a while, but tried to wait it out until she felt normal again.

Over the next hour Jasmine helped Taylor consider what she'd done, in ways she'd never thought of before. She helped her understand what it means to know, grieve, and confess her sin to God.

See Your Sin against God

Immediately after Adam and Eve tasted the forbidden fruit, its sweetness wore off. The aftertaste of regret was more bitter than they could've imagined. Shame and fear drove them to cover themselves and hide from God in the shadows of Eden's tree line.

Into the darkness God cried out, "Where are you?" God's first question to humanity wasn't seeking information. He knew where they were. His question was an act of mercy intended to draw them out of hiding and into his light. God desired reconciliation, but it couldn't come until they owned up to what they'd done.

Becoming aware of our sin does not happen naturally. We may feel its effects, but seeing it for what it truly is—an offense against God—is a supernatural gift. Through conversion, the Holy Spirit gives us eyes to see Jesus as precious and to believe the promise of forgiveness. He shows us the ugliness of sin, the beauty of God's righteousness, and the dread of coming judgment (John 16:8). He unites us to Christ and immediately begins conforming us to his image. The Spirit is our Helper who enables obedience and alerts us to disobedience (John 14:26).

Conviction is an act of mercy that awakens us to our guilt before a holy God. His Spirit graciously calls, "Where are you? What are you doing here? What have you done?" Conviction helps us to realize, "Jesus would not look at these images or meditate on these thoughts or use his body to sin against this person—he gave his body for the sins I'm trying to enjoy!"

But God doesn't just want us to know we're sinners; he wants us to talk to him about it. If conviction refers to awareness of sin, confession refers to acknowledgment of it. *Confession* means "agreement," and so to confess means to agree with God that we've sinned and done what is evil in his sight.[1] Purity of heart depends on confession of sin.

In Christ we enjoy a secure relationship with God that is nonetheless kept vibrant through confession. He doesn't merely want us to feel bad for our sin. Remorse without repentance is like hearing a diagnosis of disease but seeking no remedy.

Resisting the Spirit's call to confess marks the path of those who don't inherit salvation. Adding a spoonful of concrete to a bucket of water seems inconsequential. But if spoonful after spoonful is added, and none removed, the bucket will become an impenetrable block. Harboring sin is one of the surest ways to harden your heart against God.

Unconfessed sin says to the living God, "Hush, Lord. I love my sin. I care more about enjoying it than pleasing you. You may *not* have your way with me." Conviction is his mercy, but callousness his judgment. Let us take seriously the repeated warning: "If you hear his voice, do not harden your hearts" (Heb. 3:7–8, 15; 4:7; see Ps. 95:7–11).

Some of us have very sensitive consciences and can be crippled by such warnings. Our prayer sounds more like, "Lord, I've offended

---

1   There are various Hebrew words for *confess*, but one of the most often used is *yada'*, which means "to show, point out, or make known," depending on its form (see Ps. 32:5; Prov. 28:13); W. Gesenius and S. P. Tregelles, *Gesenius' Hebrew and Chaldee Lexicon to the Old Testament Scriptures* (Bellingham, WA: Faithlife, 2003), 332, Logos Bible software.

    In Greek, the primary words are *homologeo* and *exomologeo*, which mean "to say the same thing, to agree, to admit, to acknowledge" (see James 5:16; 1 John 1:9); G. Kittel, G. Friedrich, and G. W. Bromiley, *Theological Dictionary of the New Testament* (Grand Rapids, MI: Eerdmans, 1985), 687.

you so many times already this morning that if I confessed everything, I don't know if I'd have time to do anything else today!" We should praise God for sensitivity to sin, but we must also ask for help to not become crippled by excessive introspection.

Sometimes we vacillate between callousness and overintrospection. The conviction of the Spirit is not meant to condemn, or merely suggest a little change. Conviction is a merciful summons to see your sin against Jesus and your need to repent. It is a call to step into the light of his mercy and openly declare what you have done. Proverbs 28:13 assures us,

> Whoever conceals his transgressions will not prosper,
>   but he who confesses and forsakes them will obtain mercy.

Despite God's promise of mercy, fear will tempt you to keep your compromises hidden, to fight being exposed. Though we may preserve our facade for a while, the cost is great. We distance ourselves from the Lord. We slow down our sanctification.[2] Though crushing at times, God convicts us "for our good, that we may share his holiness" (Ps. 32:3–4; Heb. 12:10–11).

But the Spirit does not just want us to feel conviction and speak confession; he wants us to feel the weight of what we have done.

Grieve Your Sin against God

One Native American tradition teaches that inside each person's heart is a triangle. When someone does evil, the gods turn the triangle and its edges prick the heart, alerting them to stop. But if the pricking is ignored, the edges eventually wear down, leaving

---

2 John 3:20; Rom. 8:29; 2 Cor. 3:18; Eph. 1:3–6.

an endlessly spinning circle in a calloused, unfeeling heart. While the seared conscience of an unbeliever is tragic, the Bible paints an even more severe picture of a believer's sin.

Christians sin with spiritual eyes wide open and hearts brimming with knowledge of God's grace and glory. In a sense, this makes our sin even more grievous to God than that of an unbeliever. We don't simply reject an unknown deity; we forsake the God who united us with himself with covenantal love. This is why James likens our sin to adultery: "You adulterous people! Do you not know that friendship with the world is enmity with God?" (James 4:4). Would you be grieved if your spouse paraded his or her adulterous lover around your home? How much more is God's Spirit grieved when we enjoy lustful lovers with the body he indwells. Secret sin on earth is open adultery before heaven.

Our sin grieves God, and it ought to grieve us as well (Eph. 4:30). Thus James weds assurance of grace with an appeal to grieve:

> He gives more grace. Therefore it says, "God opposes the proud but gives grace to the humble." Submit yourselves therefore to God. Resist the devil, and he will flee from you. Draw near to God, and he will draw near to you. Cleanse your hands, you sinners, and purify your hearts, you double-minded. Be wretched and mourn and weep. Let your laughter be turned to mourning and your joy to gloom. Humble yourselves before the Lord, and he will exalt you. (James 4:6–10)

Pride minimizes sin, but humility mourns it. The gravity of sin—and the danger it does to our soul, our family, our church, and God's name and kingdom—calls for mourning. As pastor Ed Moore once said to me, "If your sin has not crushed your spirit, there is a good chance your repentance will be shallow, and it won't be long before you go right back to it." This may sound antigospel at first, but too often we run to find comfort for sin before taking time to grieve it. I'm not urging you to beat yourself up with antigospel penance. Our tears cannot wash away our sin; only Jesus's blood can do that. But true tears of repentance testify to a heart that's been appropriately broken due to its adulterous betrayal.

We need divine grace to help us rightly grieve. Bring the command you've broken to the Lord; plead with him to break your heart over what breaks his. Pray something like, *Father, this is your word I dismissed. This is your command I transgressed. I wanted to please myself with sin more than I wanted to please you. Help me to feel righteous grief.* This is not morbid reflection; it's a heart-purifying response that helps us to see God. Draw near to him with mourning, and trust that he will comfort you with his presence (Matt. 5:4; James 4:8). The beautiful diamond of his grace shines brightest when laid on the black velvet backdrop of our guilt.

Pray also that God would help you to be grieved over your sin against him—not just its consequences. This distinction is essential, for "godly grief produces a repentance that leads to salvation without regret, whereas worldly grief produces death" (2 Cor. 7:10). Godly grief prepares our heart for repentance; worldly grief keeps the focus on ourselves. Godly grief shifts our focus vertically, to see our sin piercing Christ on the cross; worldly grief is concerned with damage control, attempting to put out the dumpster fire our sin has caused.[3]

3 For extended meditation on how believers ought to grieve their sin, read John Owen, *The Mortification of Sin*, 3rd ed. (Edinburgh, UK: Banner of Truth, 2004), 66–72. For more tender counsel, consider Donald Whitney's article "Grieve over Sin So You Can Grow," Crosswalk.com, February 22, 2002, www.crosswalk.com/newsletters-only/live-it/grieve-over-sin-so-you-can-grow-1122108.html.

Yet as you grieve, don't do so as one condemned. Grieve with this despair-slaying promise guarding your heart: "There is therefore now no condemnation for those who are in Christ Jesus" (Rom. 8:1). We grieve as those loved by the one we have sinned against. Godly grief, then, treasures this promise: "If we say we have no sin, we deceive ourselves, and the truth is not in us. If we confess our sins, he is faithful and just to forgive us our sins and to cleanse us from all unrighteousness" (1 John 1:8–9).

God alone can forgive sins, and he delights in doing so for all who flee to the risen Savior.

Confess Your Sin to God

Because confessing sin isn't natural to us, the Holy Spirit helps us apply the Scripture to ourselves. He helps us pray in the need of the moment, and teaches us to shape our words to God according to God's words to us.[4] Over the years I've made a list of passages that model confession, and I often use them to bring my sin to God.[5] Psalm 51 is one that I regularly revisit.

David wrote this psalm after the prophet Nathan confronted him about his hidden sins of exploitation and murder. This backdrop has often aided my prayers because I know David's words were birthed from not only the Spirit's inspiration, but also personal grief. What follows are portions of a personal confession after indulging with pornography years ago.

Have mercy on me, O God,
    according to your steadfast love;

---

4   See, for example, Ps.119:18, 36; Acts 4:24–26; Rom. 8:26–27; Eph. 6:18.

5   I most regularly turn to Pss. 32; 38; 51; 103; 130, and 1 John 1:5–10. Other helpful passages include Lev. 26:40–45; Josh. 7:18–21; 2 Sam. 24:10–14; Neh. 1:4–11; Luke 15:11–32; 18:9–13.

according to your abundant mercy
   blot out my transgressions.
Wash me thoroughly from my iniquity,
   and cleanse me from my sin! (Ps. 51:1–2)

God, have mercy on me. Please do not give me what I deserve. Your love has been steadfast, but mine has not. My heart and mind are filled with sinful replays. According to your abundant mercy blot out . . . scrub out . . . tear out the stains of my transgression. Cleanse my sin; it runs so deeply in me.

For I know my transgressions,
   and my sin is ever before me.
Against you, you only, have I sinned
   and done what is evil in your sight,
so that you may be justified in your words
   and blameless in your judgment. (Ps. 51:3–4)

I cannot stop thinking about my sin. Images haunt me. I have sinned against others, but supremely against you. Your holy eyes saw my desires and my deceit. I did in full view of you what I would never do before another person. I grieved you by giving myself to another lover. You have every right to crush and condemn me. I plead for mercy. I believe Jesus was crushed and condemned for me. His blood is my only boast. Cover my sins; do not count them against me.

Create in me a clean heart, O God,
   and renew a right spirit within me.
Cast me not away from your presence,

and take not your Holy Spirit from me.[6]
Restore to me the joy of your salvation,
    and uphold me with a willing spirit. (Ps. 51:10–12)

At times I love what you hate and remain unmoved by what you love. I can be so fickle, Lord; please change my heart. Fill me with your Spirit. Do not withhold your merciful presence from me. God, give me your joy, and a heart that desires to obey you at all times. Keep me sober-minded and don't allow me to forget this grief the next time I'm tempted. Make me like Jesus.

Once you've grieved and confessed your sin to God, don't dwell on it. Instead, draw near to his throne of grace to receive healing mercy.[7]

The Fruit of Confession
Confession Restores Fellowship
If all my sins are forgiven in Christ, a believer may wonder, *why do I need to confess my sins to God?*

Our *relationship* with God as his children was established when we were born again. But our *fellowship* with God can ebb and flow based on our obedience. Through *union* with Christ by faith, we stand justified in his righteousness and there is nothing we, or anyone else, can do to remove that from us.[8] Our *communion*

---

6 David's prayer, "Take not your Holy Spirit from me," has terrified many believers who are afraid of losing their salvation due to their sin. We must understand, however, that David's prayer is a plea for God to not remove his Spirit from empowering him as king. Under the new covenant, the Holy Spirit seals believers until the day of redemption. We cannot lose what Christ has freely given to us (Eph. 1:13–14; 4:30).

7 Chapter 11 explores the invitation of Heb. 4:14–16 more deeply.

8 See John 1:12–13; 10:28–29; Rom. 5:1–11; 8:29–39.

with Christ, however, can more or less please him depending on whether or not we obey.

Human relationships function similarly. My children will always be my children, no matter what they do. But the quality of our fellowship depends greatly on how we relate to one another. They will sin against me and I will sin against them—but we will always be family. Thankfully, we have a Father in heaven who never sins against us.

The only right response to God's steadfast love is to trust and obey him in order to please him.[9] Striving to obey him springs from faith-filled joy in his love. Though sin does not break our relationship with God, it does affect our fellowship with him. It pushes him away. It grieves his heart. It creates temporary obstacles to our communion. A faithful response to sin, then, involves drawing near to God in faith through confession, repentance, and trusting the forgiveness of Jesus Christ.

Since fellowship with God is precious, don't delay your confessions. Learn to keep short accounts with God. Healthy fellowship is sustained by frequent confession. Sometimes these will be short prayers, but we can also benefit from prolonged periods of focused prayer. As you confess, keep the enjoyment of fellowship with him central.

Confessing in this way purifies our hearts, deepens our humility, maintains our fellowship, and enables us to see the glory of Jesus all the more clearly. Repentance does not just give us a clear conscience before God; it also deepens our fellowship and grows us in holiness.

Confession Fosters Fear

In our flesh, we naturally fear the consequences of sin without actually fearing the God we offend. Scripture corrects this thinking:

---

9 See Rom. 12:1; 2 Cor. 5:9; Gal. 1:10; Eph. 5:10; Phil. 4:8; Col. 1:10; 1 Thess. 2:4; Heb. 11:6.

If you, O LORD, should mark iniquities,
    O Lord, who could stand?
But with you there is forgiveness,
    that you may be feared. (Ps. 130:3–4)

Receiving forgiveness cultivates proper fear. Left to ourselves, we could not stand; if God were merely fair, he would strike us down. Yet in mercy he struck Christ instead and raised us with him. Seeing the cost of our forgiveness moves us to want to resist sin.

The devil knows his sin and trembles before God—but not with a fear leading to repentance. Those who have been forgiven, however, are freed to fear God rightly. For worshipful fear is not paralyzing, but tenderizing. A heart that shrugs at forgiveness reveals flippancy, not saving fear. But for those for whom sin is bitter, Christ is wonderfully sweet. Forgiveness restrains us from sin by cultivating reverence for the forgiver.

Confession Stirs Thankfulness

Confessing to God brings us face to face with the one who knows us fully, yet forgives us completely. Forgiveness produces thankfulness. As Jesus taught, the one who has been forgiven much loves much (Luke 7:47).

The connection between sexual purity and gratitude is clear: "Sexual immorality and all impurity or covetousness must not even be named among you, as is proper among saints. Let there be no filthiness nor foolish talk nor crude joking, which are out of place, but instead let there be thanksgiving" (Eph. 5:3–4).

When discontented with what God has given, we become susceptible to immorality. When content with the gifts of God, however, we become less prone to indulge in the passing pleasures of sin.

A grumbling heart feels justified in sinful escapes, but a thankful one finds contentment in whatever God provides. Though mere willpower cannot produce thankfulness, meditating on Calvary can. Arnold Dallimore observes:

> When we think too lightly of sin, we think too lightly of the Savior. He who has stood before his God, convicted and condemned, with the rope about his neck, is the man to weep for joy when he is pardoned, to hate the evil which has been forgiven him, and to live to the honor of the Redeemer by whose blood he has been cleansed.[10]

Meditate on the assurance of God's love for you. Neither demon nor disaster can pry you from Christ's grasp. His love is an everlasting love that was never earned and therefore can never be lost. Christ has called you and he will keep you (John 10:28–30; Rom. 8:28–39).

Thankfulness lifts our eyes from the disappointment of being single, the difficulty of marriage, the pressures of work, or the despair of broken dreams—and sets them on Christ who gave us everything when he gave us himself.

Take unhurried time, then, to honestly confess. There are no small, safe sins. But there is a good and gracious God. Pray the words of David:

> Search me, O God, and know my heart!
>> Try me and know my thoughts!
> And see if there be any grievous way in me,
>> and lead me in the way everlasting! (Ps. 139:23–24)

10 Arnold A. Dallimore, *Spurgeon: A Biography* (Carlisle, PA: Banner of Truth, 1985), 14.

9

Drop the Facade

"I AM SO AFRAID."

Brian's normally intimidating frame had been reduced to a puddle. The military captain stood in my office, having just confessed a string of adulterous affairs, and was trying to figure out how to tell his wife.

Leaning back with a sunken stare, he said: "I've flown over sixty missions in enemy territory. I've been in firefights and had missiles shot at me. But all that seems so much easier than telling her what I've done."

The fear of confessing sin can be paralyzing, and sometimes seems even worse than dying.

I remember wanting to be free—by any means besides complete honesty. I fought it with every excuse imaginable. I thought, *God, I've confessed everything to you. You know I love you. I'll never do this again . . . but if I do, then I'll confess to someone else.*

Sin assures us that we're safe behind the mask of lies, but we're not. We scramble to disconnect being honest with God about our sin from the need to be honest with others, too. And in that dark void, we change. We start to tell lies, and eventually believe them. We resist the Spirit's nudges and quench his convicting voice. Slowly, living with hidden lies becomes normal.

Confessing sin to another believer rips off the mask of hypocrisy so we can breathe the air of honesty. It enlivens our heart to feel again, and it removes the veil so we can see Christ afresh. Confession humbles us, which by nature uproots the pride that keeps immorality alive and attractive to our souls.

Our hope for change lies in seeing Christ, but we will never see him until we step into the light and confess our sin to others.

Confess Your Sin to Others

James 5:16 clearly says, "Confess your sins to one another and pray for one another, that you may be healed." God assures us that while our relationship with him is personal, it is not private. Because we are a body, what we do in our personal lives affects our brothers and sisters in Christ. Knit together by the Holy Spirit, how we live affects the rest of the body. How, then, can we speak the truth to one another "in love" and "not lie to one another" if we don't speak honestly about our sins (Eph. 4:25; Col. 3:9)?

Some suggest that if we confess our sins to God, we don't need to confess to others. While this may be true at times, the overwhelming witness of Scripture is plain:

If we say we have fellowship with him while we walk in darkness, we lie and do not practice the truth. But if we walk in the light, as he is in the light, we have fellowship with one another, and the blood of Jesus his Son cleanses us from all sin. (1 John 1:6–7)

Fellowship with God and others is founded on walking in the light with God and others.

Are you walking in the light? Who knows your intimate temptations and sins?

If no one in your life knows your weaknesses, temptations, and sin patterns, then you are in danger. If no believer hears your confession, then you remain alone in your sin, apart from God, which is a dreadful place to be. Fellow believers are God's gifts to help you fight sin and endure in faith. As you pursue wise accountability relationships, then, bear in mind the following principles.

Confess to a Small Circle of Friends

It's both unwise and unnecessary to be fully and equally transparent with everyone, but we should be brutally honest with some trusted friends (Prov. 18:24). By sharing with a few close friends consistently, you provide a realistic picture of your pursuit of holiness. Their prayers can then be more informed and their counsel more specific.

It is easy and dangerous to hide your sin in a crowd, but a close circle of trusted friends provides safety for your soul.

Discerning who should be privy to this most intimate part of your life is vital. Develop relationships with people you can see face to face. An old buddy in another town whom you Skype with once a month is not the answer. Face-to-face confessions personalize our sin, and freshly shock us with the reality that our sins are not abstract in nature, but personal. Choose someone who is mature in Christ, who can be trusted with life details, who will battle for you in prayer, and who preferably is in your church.[1]

---

1 See chapter 7 for a refresher on this kind of community.

Share Your Temptations

Temptation is not sin, but it is dangerous. Learning to reach out to close friends when you're tempted is an essential part of resisting. Secrecy strengthens sin; light saps it. Keeping your struggle quiet can seem attractive, since it lets you nibble a little longer before you flee. But sin is never satisfied. If you feed it, it only grows stronger. If you don't want to fall off sin's cliff, don't walk along temptation's edge.

Confess Sins Quickly

The longer you wait to confess, the more likely it becomes that you never will. In my accountability relationships I promise to confess any compromise within twenty-four hours, though I try to within minutes. Sin is a cancer—it must be rooted out as quickly as possible before it spreads.

Confess Sins Honestly

If you do sin, you will be tempted to lie about it. The command to speak the truth to one another demands our confessions be honest (Eph. 4:15). We must learn to confess specific sins specifically. Don't hover in generalities: "I'm struggling" or "I had a rough few days" or "I've been tempted recently." Those are good introductions to the conversation; they're not the substance. Honest confession is straightforward:

> Last night I felt the temptation to look at sensual pictures on my phone, and I did not resist. I looked at soft and hardcore pornography on and off for about forty-five minutes. I stopped several times but kept coming back. I ended up masturbating as well. I thought about reaching out for help, but I was afraid and wanted to sin.

Be honest enough to expose the sin in your heart, but general enough to not tempt your friend's imagination by being unnecessarily graphic.

How God Uses Confession to Others

When Brian confessed his adulteries to me, sin lost a measure of power over him. This isn't because the confession itself had power, but because God used it to draw Brian to brave trust in Jesus. The Lord honored his faith and granted freedom from the shame and lust that gripped him. God uses humble, honest, and painful confession to help us see him more clearly.

God Uses Honest Confession to Humble Us

God opposes pride (James 4:6; 1 Pet. 5:5). All sin is rooted in pride, as is our quest to keep it concealed. But when we sit down with another believer and own our sin, God lovingly illuminates the grossness. Confession exposes us for who we really are, rather than who we pretend to be.

How does your desire to impress others hinder honest confession?

So often we want to be thought well of by others, even if it means dishonoring God. This is why we dress up our sin and leave out incriminating details. Concealment feeds pride, but confession cuts its throat.

Dietrich Bonhoeffer describes it well:

> Confession in the presence of a brother [or sister] is the profoundest kind of humiliation. It hurts, it cuts a man down, it is a dreadful blow to pride. . . . In the confession of concrete sins the old man dies a painful, shameful death before the eyes of a brother. Because this humiliation is so hard, we continually

scheme to avoid it. Yet in the deep mental and physical pain of humiliation before a brother we experience our rescue and salvation.[2]

When we fear people more than God, we fall into a deadly snare. But few things slay cowardice and pride like sitting down with a trusted believer and saying, "Here is what I have done; please pray for me and remind me of God's promises."

God Uses Honest Confession to Sober Us

As drunkenness disorients the body, sin disorients the soul. When people are drunk, they behave in a clumsy way because their perception of reality is altered. In the same way, coddling sin distorts reality. We sin privately in ways we never would if our parents, spouse, or church friends were watching. Meanwhile, all of it is done in full view of an all-seeing, all-knowing God.

Holy sobriety is heightened when we confess to those we've sinned against. Have you ever seen a wife tell her husband that she's been unfaithful? A husband confess to his wife that he's been looking at pornography? The pain and sorrow are beyond words.

Facing the consequences of our sin is one of the greatest deterrents to confessing it. But hear these two truths. First, *you can trust God with the consequences of your confession.* If he is able to use history's greatest evil—the crucifixion of his Son—as history's greatest good, then he can handle the fallout from your sin. Second, *being clean before God in devastation is better than being cut off from him in a mirage of deceit.* Hiding sin stokes a

---

2   Dietrich Bonheoffer, *Life Together* (San Francisco: HarperOne, 2009), 114.

crushing anxiety that is always terrified of being exposed.[3] Stepping into the light will be hard, but the fruit God will produce will be eternally worth it.

God Uses Honest Confession to Heal Us

We cannot sin without consequence. At times our sin can bring relational destruction, physical sickness, or even death.[4] Most consistent, though, are the spiritual consequences. When we succumb to sin, our flesh is inflamed, our peace quenched, our godly desire sapped, our joy smothered, our prayer hollowed, our resolve weakened, and our communion with God and others hindered.

God's prescription for these afflictions is honest confession and hopeful prayer. James instructs us to "confess your sins to one another and pray for one another, that you may be healed" (James 5:16). God uses confession like a surgeon to remove sin's cancer, no matter how deeply it has metastasized. The removal is painful, but not as painful as letting it remain.

Fellow believers act as priests who point us to Jesus who alone can forgive and heal our sin-inflicted wounds.[5] They have no power or authority to forgive us, but they point us to Jesus, who has both power and authority to forgive. Above all, God uses confession to clear the eyes of our soul to more clearly see Christ.

---

3 See Pss. 32:3–6; 51:8; Prov. 28:1; Acts 24:16; Titus 1:15; Heb. 10:22.

4 Not all sin leads to sickness, but some certainly can. First Corinthians 11:29–30 speaks of some believers who became sick and even died because of their sin against God and one another (see also Acts 5:1–11).

5 I am not referring to the Roman Catholic practice, which wrongly claims that ordained priests alone have been entrusted with the authority to absolve sin. Rather, God has given all believers a priestly role in which they minister to one another by directing one another's attention to Christ, who is our high priest.

When Someone Confesses to You

What happens after a confession is almost as important as the confession itself. Here are some ways to respond.

Guard Your Own Heart

"If anyone is caught in any transgression," Paul warns, "you who are spiritual should restore him in a spirit of gentleness. Keep watch on yourself, lest you too be tempted" (Gal. 6:1).

You may be tempted to curiously investigate a sin that's foreign to you, which can lead to your own ensnarement. Or you may be tempted to follow up on a detail to feed your flesh. Regardless of how spiritually mature you are, you are never beyond the reach of Satan's fiery darts.

The specific warning in Galatians 6 concerns pride. When someone shares a sin, we can be tempted toward harshness and judgmentalism (Gal. 5:15, 26). Guard yourself by considering your own sin. Though it may be different, does it not grieve God? Was Jesus not crucified for it? Yet has he not been patient and gentle and merciful with you? There are times to be tough and warn friends of sin's danger, but we must always remain tender and remind them of the Savior.

If you are the one sinned against, you may rightly feel the pain of being sinned against. Your grief is not sinful, but you must remain on guard to not respond sinfully through anger or revenge (Rom. 12:19–21; Eph. 4:26–27). Take time to process what has been shared with you, and reach out to your pastor or an experienced counselor who is able to bring the gospel to bear on your situation.

Lead the Confessor to Jesus

When friends open up about their sin, point them to Calvary, where Christ was slain in their place.[6] Lead them to the throne

---

6 Chapters 11 and 12 focus on how we can approach the throne of grace to receive help in our time of need.

of grace through prayer. Pray aloud God's promises of mercy, and call on God to keep them.[7] Plead with him to heal their body and cleanse their mind. Help them lift their burden and cast it on the Lord, knowing he cares for them (1 Pet. 5:7).

Plan the Confessor's Repentance

Once the dust has settled, help the person make a concrete plan to not repeat his or her sin. Mercy is promised to those who confess and forsake their sin (Prov. 28:13; Matt. 3:8). Remember: confession without repentance is hypocrisy. So we help our friends consider why they sinned as they did, how they got to that point, and what changes need to be put in place to ensure they don't revert. This often takes time, patience, and help from a pastor.

When Brian confessed his adulteries to his wife, it broke her heart. But God has helped them, continues to heal them, and is now using them to help others. Confessing our sin is not an end in itself, it is a means to an end—seeing the beauty of Jesus and helping others to do the same.

---

7 I encourage you to make your own list, but here are a few promises to begin with: Pss. 32; 38; 51; 104; 130; Isa. 1:18; Matt. 11:28; 1 Cor. 6:9–11; Heb. 4:14–16; James 4:6–10; 1 Pet. 2:24–25; 1 John 1:9–2:2.

10

Sin No More

MIKE BROKE HIS SILENCE as he leaned over the table: "If I'm a Christian, why do I keep doing this? We both know we'll be back here in a couple weeks having this same conversation. I'm not sure there's any reason to keep trying."

If you were sitting across the table, what would you say to Mike?

In such moments, when I'm the one across the table, I feel helpless. I want to drop a magical gospel bomb that blows back his hair and makes him shout, "That's the answer! That settled it. I'm finally free!"

In all my years of pastoral ministry, however, that's never happened. Not even close. And it won't for you, because there are no quick fixes in the war against sin. Nevertheless, the truth that Mike and every other Christian must believe is this: you don't have to obey sin anymore. This does not always *feel* true, but it *is*—because God says so in his word.

If you are in Christ, you are not who you used to be, so you do not have to do what you used to do.

Consider what the apostle Paul says:

> How can we who died to sin still live in it? . . . just as Christ was
> raised from the dead by the glory of the Father, we too might
> walk in newness of life. . . . our old self was crucified with him
> . . . so that we would no longer be enslaved to sin. . . . So you
> also must consider yourselves dead to sin and alive to God in
> Christ Jesus. Let not sin therefore reign in your mortal body, to
> make you obey its passions. Do not present your members to
> sin as instruments for unrighteousness, but present yourselves
> to God as those who have been brought from death to life, and
> your members to God as instruments for righteousness. For sin
> will have no dominion over you. (Rom. 6:2–14)

Dead to Sin

You are not who you used to be. Mike struggled to grasp this truth.
Maybe he knew it intellectually, but not experientially, not in a way
that seemed to actually help him. The itch to scroll through sensual
images can be strong. The urge to masturbate seems reasonable, if
not insatiable. The thrill of a hookup or adulterous rendezvous is
powerful.

Yet in Christ, we are free to flee. God has "delivered us from
the domain of darkness and transferred us to the kingdom of his
beloved Son" (Col. 1:13). And walking in freedom requires understanding and acting on what God has done for us in Christ.

Who You Were

We were once alive to sin and dead to God (Eph. 2:1–3). We
wanted to sin because we loved it. We suppressed truth about God
and traded him for idols that catered to our lusts (Rom. 1:18,

23). We dreamt up ways to sin and encouraged others to join (Ps. 36:4; Rom. 1:32). We isolated ourselves from people who told us the truth. We did not fear God, and we confused his patience for approval (Ps. 36:1; Rom. 2:1–4). Even when we avoided evil, our motivation was rooted in self-preservation rather than pleasing God. Sin owned even our best days.

We *had* to sin, since sin was our master.[1] And like a slave master, sin forced us to embrace our identity as slaves. *You are a porn addict. You are gay. You are a failure. You are unwanted. You are a cheater. You will never be free.* Sin demoralized us and stole any hope of escape. Perhaps it even told us our slavery was liberty: *You have the right to do whatever you want with your body. Anyone who doesn't affirm your choices is your enemy.*

Have you heard these lies? Believed them? Slavery to sin isn't just a theory about human trouble; it's the reality of our condition apart from Christ. Sin controls not only what we do, but how we see God, ourselves, and others. It shapes our view of our bodies and our sexuality. Sin makes us think we're free, when in fact we're not. It makes us think we're on the road to happiness, when in fact we're headed for destruction.

Who You Are

You were dead in the trespasses and sins in which you once walked . . . and were by nature children of wrath. . . . But God, being rich in mercy, because of the great love with which he loved us, even when we were dead in our trespasses, made us alive together with Christ. (Eph. 2:1–5)

---

1 See Rom. 8:6–9; 2 Tim. 2:26. For a helpful study on our love for and slavery to sin, see *Freedom of the Will* by Jonathan Edwards and *Bondage of the Will* by Martin Luther. These brothers approach the subject from different angles, but arrive at similar conclusions.

"But God" is one of the sweetest phrases ever uttered. It turns the spotlight from our hopeless slavery to our healing Savior. We were dead, *but God* rescued us.[2] We were enslaved, *but God* bound our oppressor. We were far off, *but God* brought us near. Jesus was buried, *but God* raised him again.[3]

What makes this good news is that Jesus did this *for* us. Through faith we are united with Jesus and given both new life and a new identity. Positionally, we *stand* accepted by God's grace; practically, we *step* as liberated children loved by God. If we are in Christ, we are brand-new creations (2 Cor. 5:17).[4]

Of course, our union with Jesus doesn't immediately extinguish all sinful desires. Far from it. Sin tempts us to think like we're still slaves. But in Christ, we have been given innumerable heavenly blessings to oppose it. We are clothed in his righteousness, sealed by his Spirit, forgiven of every sin, secure in his love.[5]

In Christ, we have been delivered from sin's penalty. We will not face God's wrath, since Jesus took it for us (1 Thess. 1:10; 5:9). We're also being liberated from sin's power. We don't have to yield to it any longer, since Jesus is our Lord (Rom. 6:15–23; 1 Cor. 6:19–20). And someday we will be delivered from sin's presence. When Jesus returns, he will glorify our bodies and set us free to sin no more.

We are free from sin because we are united to Jesus. What is true of Jesus is true of us.[6] He died *for* sin; we have died *to* sin. He was

2 See Eph. 2:4–5, 12–13; Rom. 5:8; Titus 3:5; Heb. 2:15.
3 Luke 11:21–22; Acts 2:24; Eph. 2:13.
4 The phrase "in Christ," or some derivation of it, appears over 150 times in the New Testament. God continually reminds believers of their union with Jesus because they are so often tempted to forget it.
5 See John 10:29; Acts 10:43; Rom. 4:5; 8:28–39; 2 Cor. 5:21; Gal. 5:16–26; Eph. 1:3, 7, 13–14; 4:30; Heb. 8:12; 9:22; 13:5; 10:18; 1 John 1:7–9.
6 This does not mean, as Mormons or some prosperity teachers say, that we actually become little gods. That is blasphemy. Rather, through union with Christ, we partake of God's life, as a branch does a vine, and produce the fruit of godliness.

raised from the dead; we have been raised spiritually as we await the final resurrection. He ascended to sit at the Father's side; we are seated with him, too. He is raised to live forevermore; we are alive to walk in new life.[7]

The gospel of Jesus does not just free us from hell *someday*; it can also free us from sin *today*.

It's true that we are to be pitied if our hope in Christ affects only this life (1 Cor. 15:19). But we are also to be pitied if it affects only the life to come. If there is no good news for Mike, or you, or me as we fight sin today, then we might as well quit. But there is good news—and our union with Jesus has just as much a miraculous effect today as it will on that last day, when he pulls our bodies from the grave.

Union with the Savior liberates us from slavery to sin. Again: we are not who we used to be, so we do not have to do what we used to do.

As union with sin produced a slave identity, so union with Christ produces a new identity. Your old self is dead. You are alive to God. You are eternally loved. You belong to God. You are forgiven. You are blessed. You are delighted in. Your life is so united to Christ's that he will not appear in glory apart from you (Col. 3:4).[8]

You are in Christ, and he is in you. You *can* become like him. You *will* become like him. No matter how faintly his beauty flickers in your corrupted body now—plead that God and others would help you see it. And as you catch glimpses of his grace in your life, know they are the firstfruits of God's eternal purpose to make you like his Son.[9]

7 See Rom. 6:2, 6–9; 8:11; 2 Cor. 4:14; Eph. 2:6; Col. 3:3.
8 See Sinclair Ferguson, "The Practice of Mortification," *TableTalk*, January 1, 2007, www.ligonier.org/learn/articles/practice-mortification/.
9 For a wonderful reflection on this truth, read J. R. Miller's sermon "Transformed by Beholding," 1888.

Free to Obey

Because God loves and accepts you, you are free to obey him. Free to stop giving in to sin. Free to confess your failures and allow others to see your flaws—because God has already paid your debt in full.

What does this mean? For starters, you no longer wear the serial number of sin's death camp. You have been liberated. You have been granted citizenship in God's kingdom. You have been adopted as God's child. You are clothed in Christ's righteousness. You are loved by God, sealed by his Spirit, washed by Christ's blood.

Christians in the Bible are never defined by their sin. They have a new nature and new identity. This is why "gay Christian" or "adulterous Christian" are unhelpful identity markers. God never refers to believers by their sin or temptations; he refers to them according to their union with Jesus. We are *saints*, set apart from sin's dominion.[10]

While believers are no longer enslaved to sin, we must remain vigilant lest we become ensnared in sin. The story of Lot is a sobering example. Lot was Abram's nephew who joined Abram as he followed God. Yet Lot chose to make his home in a wicked city. Tragically, Sodom made its home in him as well. Lot had been drawn by the city's beauty, and he remained in it, despite its effect on him (Gen. 13:10; 19:1–38). Though he was "righteous," his "soul was tormented" (1 Cor. 10:13; 2 Pet. 2:7–10). Lot chose to move there, remain there, and linger despite angelic warnings. He was delivered, but at great cost.[11]

---

10 *Saints* is the most common name used to describe Christians in the New Testament. The word *saint* means "holy one." Christians are nowhere called "sinners" in the New Testament. Saints do sin, but it's essential to understand that our identity is defined by our set-apartness in Christ, not our ongoing battle with indwelling sin.

11 You would be blessed to read J. C. Ryle's sermon on Jesus's warning, "Remember Lot's Wife" (Luke 17:32).

While believers are free from sin, we can still become deeply ensnared or entangled in it. But such ensnarement is a *choice*; sin has no power to *make* a believer do anything. Nevertheless, if believers continually give in to temptation and grieve the Holy Spirit, their flesh will strengthen and their hearts will harden.

This is what Mike was experiencing. He consciously, repeatedly, intentionally made sinful compromises. He grieved and quenched the Spirit. He fed and stoked his flesh. As his affections for sin warmed, his affections for Jesus cooled. With the Spirit's resurrecting power hushed, his liberated identity ignored, and his sinful flesh enflamed, Mike *felt* enslaved, even though he was actually free. The doors of the prison were open, but he chose to remain in his cell.

Hebrews 12:1 exhorts believers to throw aside "the sin that so easily entangles." The word *entangle* was used of wrestlers in a coliseum who encircled an opponent's legs to take them down. It can also be translated "beset." A "besetting sin" is a unique area of weakness in which we feel particularly susceptible to succumb when tempted. But when we *choose* to give in, we allow it to entangle us.

Never grow comfortable, then, with any sin. Small sins are just great ones in disguise. Any sin allowed to remain will prove to be a metastasizing cancer for your soul. Sin is imperialistic. It may seem slow at first, but this is part of its deceitful plan.

Friend, never be comforted by how much worse of a sinner you could be. No sin is safe, no matter how small you perceive it. This is why the Bible's warnings to believers are so severe. Consider, for example, Ephesians 5:5–6: "Be sure of this, that everyone who is sexually immoral or impure, or who is covetous (that is, an idolater), has no inheritance in the kingdom of Christ and God. Let no one deceive you with empty words, for because of these things the wrath of God comes upon the sons of disobedience."

Such warnings are not hypothetical scare tactics. God gives real warnings to humble our heart, sober our mind, provoke repentance, and make us cling to Jesus. Take time to read the biblical warnings, and ask God to give you sobriety.[12]

You Do Not Have to Sin Anymore

Years ago in Florida, an elderly woman was picked up at a shopping mall and placed in a local psychiatric institution. She was known for scrounging through garbage cans and hoarding what she found in her car and two-bedroom apartment. In an attempt to identify her, detectives sifted through her belongings. What they found was shocking.

According to bank books, stock securities, oil drilling rights, and land holdings scattered throughout her possessions, they discovered that she was the heir of an inheritance worth millions of dollars. Tragically, she had lived for years in poverty—despite having more money than she could need at her disposal.[13]

Many believers live like this woman. We have a wealth of grace from God, yet we leave it unclaimed. But it's not too late for that to change.

So you also must consider yourselves dead to sin and alive to God in Christ Jesus. Let not sin therefore reign in your mortal body, to make you obey its passions. Do not present your

---

12 We do well to study the New Testament's *warnings against abiding in sin* (1 Cor. 6:9–11; Gal. 5:19–21; Heb. 3:13; 5:11–6:9; 10:19–31; 13:4; James 4:4; 1 John 3:9; 5:18; Rev. 2–3), along with its *exhortations for perseverance* (Matt. 5:13; 24:13; John 8:31; 15:6; Rom. 11:22; 1 Cor. 9:27; 10:12; 15:1; Col. 1:22–23; 1 Tim. 4:1; 2 Tim. 2:12; 1 John 2:19; 2 John 1:9; Jude 20; Rev. 14:12; 21:7).

13 "'Derelict' Called Illinois Heiress," *The New York Times*, February 25, 1977, www.nytimes.com/1977/02/25/archives/derelict-called-illinois-heiress.html/.

members to sin as instruments for unrighteousness, but present yourselves to God as those who have been brought from death to life, and your members to God as instruments for righteousness. (Rom. 6:11–13)

Let's conclude this chapter by drawing three lessons from this passage.

1. Consider the Truth

To "consider" or "reckon" that we are dead to sin and alive to God is the first command we find in the book of Romans (Rom. 6:11). To "consider" means to keep a record of something for the purpose of acting on it later.[14] God tells us four times in Romans 6:1–10 to know and believe certain truths; here we're commanded to continually believe them. As a married woman can look to her ring and consider herself unavailable for dating, so we look to Christ and consider ourselves unavailable for sin.

Ancient Israel was commanded to put God's words on their heart and also bind them on their hands, put them between their eyes, and post them on their doors—so that everywhere they went, they would consider his word (Deut. 6:1–9).[15] Similarly, our "considering" should be a continual, moment-by-moment mindset of being dead to sin and alive to God.[16] Begin your days, then, by considering God's new mercies (Lam. 3:20–26). When lust requests a rendezvous, consider: "I have been crucified with Christ"

---

14 J. P. Louw and E. A. Nida, *Greek-English Lexicon of the New Testament*, 2nd ed., vol. 1 (New York: United Bible Societies, 1996), 345.

15 In Hos. 4:6 God says Israel was destroyed for lack of knowledge. He had given them truth, but they had intentionally pushed it away, to their peril.

16 The word *consider* is in the present imperative form ("imperative" means that it's a command; "present" means that it's an ongoing action).

(Gal. 2:20). When sexual sin promises to satisfy, consider: "Only the righteousness of Christ will satisfy me" (Matt. 5:6). When a tempting situation lies ahead, consider: "I will make no provision for my flesh" (Rom. 13:14).

2. Forbid Sin to Reign

Sin wants to reclaim rule over you, but Scripture is clear: "Let not sin therefore reign in your mortal body, to make you obey its passions" (Rom. 6:12). Sin wants your body to fulfill its passions, your eyes to gaze on perversion, your hands to reach for what's not yours, your mind to be a playground for forbidden fantasies.

When sin calls, which it will, what are you going to say? Here's what: "No! You're dead to me; I'm dead to you. I'm united to Christ. I'm not your slave anymore." Imagine if a former employer called you next Saturday morning and said, "We need you to come in, make coffee, make copies, and deliver a few packages." You'd say, "No. I don't work for you anymore."

When sin says, "You deserve a break; enjoy the excitement of a quick internet search," you say, "No! You're dead to me. I'm united with Christ, who promises satisfaction." When sin says, "You're such a prude for not giving your boyfriend (or girlfriend) your body," you say, "No! My body belongs to God, as a living sacrifice. Help me, Jesus!"

You don't have to do what you used to do, because you aren't who you used to be.

3. Present Your Body to God

Though your body is affected by the fall, it is not evil. It is a neutral "instrument" that you "present" either to sin for its purposes, or to God for his pleasure (Rom. 6:13). The word *present*—meaning "to offer, dedicate, make available"—is the same word used in Romans 12:1: "Present your bodies as a living sacrifice . . . to God, which is your spiritual worship."

Not only is it worshipful to offer your body to God, it's also a joy-producing duty. Elsewhere, Paul explains: "Do you not know that your body is a temple of the Holy Spirit within you, whom you have from God? You are not your own, for you were bought with a price. So glorify God in your body" (1 Cor. 6:19–20).

Jesus shed his blood to purchase your body as a temple. And his Spirit gives you power to present your body to God. You don't have to give your eyes to that wicked show. You don't have to give your fingers to click on that link. You don't have to unite your body in that sinful relationship. Sin will say, "You should, you must, you will." But Jesus insists your old man was crucified with him and lies dead in the grave. Sin will say, "I'll give you so much pleasure." But Jesus proclaims that true joy and satisfaction come through obedience to him (John 15:1–11).

Look to Jesus. Consider who God has made you, forbid sin to rule you, and present yourself as a sacrifice of worship. You are free to do this. Remember: you don't have to do what you used to do, because you are not who you used to be.

11

Slay Your Foe

A TRAGIC HEADLINE SURFACES every so often: "Unsuspecting Owner Killed by Pet Anaconda." Everything was fine, it seemed, until the snake escaped, slithered into a bedroom, and consumed a sleeping victim.

Some of us treat sin this way. Sure, we know it can be dangerous, but we assume we can domesticate and control it. Perhaps sin plays along for a little while, appearing subdued, but it will always seek an opportunity to strike.

Though we have been freed from sin's slavery, our flesh still seeks opportunities to indulge in evil. Therefore God commands, "Put to death therefore what is earthly in you: sexual immorality, impurity, passion, evil desire, and covetousness, which is idolatry" (Col. 3:5). Sin refuses to be caged or coddled; it must be killed. It will accept no peace treaty. Hence John Owen's classic warning: "Be killing sin or it will be killing you."[1]

1 John Owen, *The Mortification of Sin*, 3rd ed. (Edinburgh, UK: Banner of Truth, 2004), chap. 2.

The steps you take in the battle against sin are a matter of life and death: "If you live according to the flesh you will die, but if by the Spirit you put to death the deeds of the body, you will live" (Rom. 8:13). The stakes could not be higher. Sin has no desire to cohabitate. It intends to dominate.

The apostle Peter pleads with us: "Abstain from the passions of the flesh, which wage war against your soul" (1 Pet. 2:11). As long as we are in this world, sin will try to sap our love for God and stoke our love for sin. We must do whatever it takes, therefore, to put it to death. Kill your love for sin, or sin will kill your love for God.[2]

The Battle Is Costly

It was late summer when Samson Parker started picking a load of corn at his nearby farm. The machine jammed. As he worked to free the impediment, the rollers grabbed his glove and sucked his hand into the gears. Sparks flew from the grinding gears, igniting dried stalks on the ground. As flames raged around him, Parker knew he only had one option.

He reached for his pocketknife, and began the grueling task of severing his right hand at the forearm. The choice was clear to him: lose his hand or lose his life. He eventually got free, made his way to his truck, and drove for help. He was airlifted to a hospital, where he was treated and eventually released.[3]

Now, why would Samson Parker cut off his hand with a pocketknife?

Everyone knows the answer. He wanted to live! He did not want to burn or bleed to death in a corn picker. He wanted to live! He

---

2 I thank God for Thomas Brooks, John Owen, and John Piper, who have helped me understand the seriousness of warfare against sin.

3 Mike Celizic, "To save his life, man cuts off arm with pocketknife," Today.com, November 26, 2007, www.today.com/news/save-his-life-man-cuts-arm-pocketknife-wbna21973683/.

wanted to kiss his wife and hug his son and be there to watch him grow up. He wanted to live, so he sawed off his hand.

Slaying sin requires drastic measures. Jesus says, "If your right eye causes you to sin, tear it out and throw it away. For it is better that you lose one of your members than that your whole body be thrown into hell. And if your right hand causes you to sin, cut it off and throw it away. For it is better that you lose one of your members than that your whole body go into hell" (Matt. 5:29–30).

Do you want to live? Do you want to escape the danger of hell? Do you want to be free from the sin that keeps you from seeing the beauty of God?

Many of us do not take Jesus seriously here. Clearly he's not promoting self-mutilation, but at the same time he is not speaking in mere hyperbole. There is something radical he intends for us to do. Jesus does not want you to literally cut off your hand, but he does want you to take extreme measures in removing sin from your life.

Are you willing to do whatever it takes to slay sin in your life?

What if it means blocking certain movie or social media sites? Or not owning a smartphone altogether? What if God wanted you to change your number or quit your job to extract yourself from an overly tempting situation? What if he asked you to break off an engagement or confess hidden sin to your spouse?

Are you willing to say yes, no matter what Jesus asks? This is part of what he meant, after all: "Whoever does not take his cross and follow me is not worthy of me" (Matt. 10:38).

Sin dies hard. It always begs for compromise. Jesus meant what he said about cutting things—sometimes drastically—out of your life.

For instance, my phone is so dumbed down that I couldn't use it to pull up a pornographic image to save my life. Only my wife and a couple trusted brothers have the code that allows me to download apps or access the internet. I have maps, music, and texting; that's about it.

Is it an inconvenience? Sure, but people lived for thousands of years without phones or apps or 24/7 internet access. And I found I couldn't live *with* it. Small compromises subtly snowballed, pushing me toward the precipice of disaster.

What intentional steps are you taking to slay sin? If you don't have a clear, specific answer, it's probably because you're not taking any. Do not keep the snake in your house. It will kill you.

The Battle Is Long

The war against sexual sin is lifelong. But though it doesn't die overnight, it can be starved. Like an enemy holed up in a fortress, we need to lay siege to sin and cut off every supply route.

Imagine being called upon to fight the greatest heavyweight UFC champion of all time. In one month, you will enter the circle and fight him until one of you yields. There is no escaping the match, but you are given one advantage. The organizers allow you to select your opponent's meal plan over the next month. You determine everything he can and cannot eat. Feed him as little or as much as you desire. What would you do?

The decision is not difficult. You would feed him a whole bunch of nothing. You would starve him so that he's woefully weak on the day of battle.

Our clash with the flesh is similar. Your flesh is a beastly opponent that only grows stronger when you feed it. This is why we must "put on the Lord Jesus Christ, and make no provision for the flesh, to gratify its desires" (Rom. 13:14).

For us to have any chance of seeing God, we must starve our sinful nature. By clicking on sensual ads or searching seductive pictures, we grieve the Spirit and feed our flesh. When we let thoughts linger and our eyes wander, we strengthen our flesh. When we entertain salacious talk or indulge romantic fantasies, we feed the beast within. And it only grows hungrier. In order to slay it, you must starve it.

What does your flesh hunger for? How do you feed it through compromise?

It isn't archaic or prudish to say no to things that hinder your walk with Jesus. Your joy is found in obedience to him, not in some television show, website, or app. Paul challenged the Corinthians to think wisely about how to use their freedoms. "All things are lawful for me," they claimed, to which Paul replied: "but not all things are helpful. . . . I will not be dominated by anything. . . . The body is not meant for sexual immorality, but for the Lord, and the Lord for the body" (1 Cor. 6:12–13). Paul wanted the Corinthians to understand that freedoms (such as what you eat, drink, and watch) must be used wisely, lest they lead you to sin. So before partaking of any form of entertainment, consider some questions:[4]

1. Does this increase my affection for Jesus?
2. Can I give God thanks for this?
3. Can I recommend this to others?
4. How might this stir up my flesh?
5. How would I know if I'm growing calloused to sin?

Watching sensual images without conviction is not a sign of spiritual maturity, but hardness of heart.

4　The first three questions were shared with me by Shai Linne during a conversation in 2013.

The Battle Is Complex

If you go to a multiplex cinema, you will sit in one theater to watch the movie you came to see. But other theaters throughout the building are showing other films. Though you aren't thinking about the other movies while you're watching yours, they are playing nonetheless.[5] This image is helpful for understanding our battle against lust. For many, this sin is the only movie playing. Our prayers are about lust; our conversations are about compromises with lust; our Bible reading is about looking for passages to help fight lust.

This approach is unhelpful in the long run.

Just as many movies are playing in a multiplex cinema, so many "sinful story lines" are playing in our lives. Pride, discontentment, envy, fear of man, anxiety, and a myriad of other vices may be raging in our flesh—but we don't notice, since we're only thinking about lust.

Purity of heart isn't about fighting just sexual sin. All sin must be slain in order to see God.

Consider Permissible Dangers

A few years back, I faced a season in which I felt particularly plagued by sexual temptation. Day after day my spirit felt weak and my flesh's hunger for sinful fulfillment felt strong. I quickly clued in key brothers, who helped me keep from going down a dark path.

One of those brothers challenged me to evaluate other ways I might be feeding my flesh. Sensuality, he explained, is not just about sexuality. We looked up the word *sensual*, which means "relating to or consisting in the gratification of the senses or the indulgence of appetite."[6] My friend then helped me perform a sobering inventory of my life.

---

5 This image is borrowed from David Powlison's wonderful article, "Sexual Sin and the Wider, Deeper Battles," *Journal of Biblical Counseling* (spring 2006), 30.

6 *Merriam-Webster*, s.v. "sensual (adj.)," accessed September 21, 2020, www.merriam-webster .com/dictionary/sensual.

I would have scorned the fools of 2 Timothy 4 who sought false teachers to tickle their ears—while overlooking the fact that I wanted everything else tickled. I was constantly checking ego-stroking or ego-deflating notifications on social media. Seemingly endless retreats to email and news highlights fed my love for distraction. Fatty foods and specialty coffee drinks became daily habits rather than disciplined treats. The excuse of tiredness fueled my retreat to movies and sports and shows each night, when I could have been running to spiritually stimulating books or songs.

My flesh was crying for a pacifier, and I was giving it what it wanted. *Though most of the things I was indulging in weren't inherently sinful, the way I was enjoying them was becoming so.* Satan's scheme was to hinder me from seeing God by smuggling in resources for my flesh in unsuspecting packages. I was sabotaging myself and didn't even realize it.

Just because you can do something does not mean you should. Something may be permissible, but we must always ask: Does this help me love God more? Does this help others love God more? Does this show God as glorious (1 Cor. 10:23–31)? What does this bring out in me? What do I desire after indulging in this?

How might you be feeding your flesh without knowing it?

Consider Inconspicuous Sins
Bianca was a women's Bible study leader active in community tutoring programs. While she never dreamed she would get involved in a sexual relationship with someone before marriage, she had. A friendship at work had taken a turn and, before Bianca knew it, she was sucked in and overwhelmed.

How did I get here? she wondered.

As we talked, we realized her sexual sin wasn't the only thing going on. She was tired of being single, hadn't planned to live in the town she was in, didn't like the career path she was following.

On top of that, she wanted people to think well of her, which pressured her to conceal her real spiritual condition. She focused on others' spiritual health while hiding her own. And underneath it all, she expressed that while she understood the Bible *said* God was good, she had a hard time believing he was really good to *her*.

There are always sins that don't seem as dangerous as sexual sin. But discontentment, bitterness, unforgiveness, anxiety, unbelief, and fear of man are cancers that, if left unattended, will grow in strength and fuel sin's war against your pursuit of God.

What sorts of inconspicuous sins might be lingering in your life? How might these be feeding your flesh and weakening you against sin's seduction?

Reasons We Don't Battle

Why do we not slay our sin? Though we know drastic measures are necessary, we often hesitate to take them. Take a moment to prayerfully examine the following reasons we resist God's summons to slay sin.

We Love Our Sin

Augustine once prayed, "Lord, make me chaste, but not yet."[7] This shockingly honest prayer reveals a love for sin that haunts many of our hearts. We desire to love God and live for him—yet we still love sin. We hate that we love it, but we love it nonetheless.

---

7 Augustine, *The Confessions of Saint Augustine*, trans. John K. Ryan (New York: Image Books, 1960), 194.

Maybe the thrill of searching for pornography gives escape from your boredom. A lover's embrace assures your worth, even if just for a night. The mysterious wonder of the forbidden fruit is just too marvelous. Whatever you love about sin, know that it is killing you. In the dark, sin tastes sweet, but the light of the beauty of Jesus reveals it to be candy-coated feces. Plead with God to change what you love.

Father, show me my sin. What am I seeking from it? Open my eyes so I can see it as you do. Change my affections that I might love to kill what you hate.

Slaying Sin Hurts

In C. S. Lewis's classic novel *The Great Divorce*, we encounter a traveler plagued by a red lizard who represents lust. The lizard sits on his shoulder, whispering in his ear, hindering him from moving toward the light. An angel asks the traveler if he wants to be rid of the pesky beast, which he answers in the affirmative. As the angel grasps the lizard by the throat, it digs in his claws, and the traveler screams, "You're hurting me now." To which the angel says, "I never said it wouldn't hurt you. I said it wouldn't kill you."[8]

If you will slay sin, it will hurt. Confession carries terrifying prospects with it. Physical withdrawals may be overbearing at the outset. A lover's heart may be broken. Shame may meet you every time you step out the door. Early in my walk as a Christian, I became ensnared in an immoral relationship, and I remember thinking that I would rather die than break it off and confess my immorality.

If you will know the freedom of seeing God, you must also know the pain of killing sin.

8 C. S. Lewis, *The Great Divorce* (New York: Simon & Schuster, 1996), 98.

Father, give me the willingness to face any pain that killing sin might bring. Do whatever it takes to free me of my lust, and give me a heart that trusts you. Use the pain to help me see you more clearly.

We Forget the Cost of Sinning

Though Israel's bodies journeyed toward the Promised Land of Canaan, their hearts were pointed back to Egypt. They looked on their former slavery with rose-colored glasses. "We remember the fish we ate in Egypt that cost nothing, the cucumbers, the melons, the leeks, the onions, and the garlic" (Num. 11:5; see Ex. 16:3). Sin tempts us to daydream about how wonderful our slavery to it was. It assures you that the pain was worth its pleasure. It lures you to linger on past perversion with fondness, even wishing you could relive it once again. Meditations like those mark the road of apostasy.

Father, help me to see my former sin as you see it. Help me to remember its bitterness instead of its sweetness. Guard me from looking back. Help me to see you and delight in what you have called me to, not what you have called me from.

If we will be freed from sin, we must be convinced that killing it will be worth it. This sort of sin-slaying faith is a gift from God. Plead with him to show you the beauty of his presence. Ask him to make you hope in the eternal pleasures reserved at his right hand. Ask him to help you have the heart of Christ who "for the joy that was set before him endured the cross, despising the shame" (Heb. 12:2).

When our desires are transformed, our resolve will be strengthened to kill any sin that might hinder us from delighting in God. Nothing is more precious than God's presence, so kill your sin before it robs you of him.

12

Embrace the Throne

THE GOLDEN THRONE of the Siamese king was just above eye level
at the end of the hall. Lofty windows welcomed sunlight, which
streamed down on the guards standing at attention. Before the
throne, visiting dignitaries knelt in respect. Servants lay prostrate
throughout the grand hall. Their elbows covered their faces to
ensure they wouldn't look on the king without permission.

The silence was interrupted when a door opened just enough
for a seven-year-old girl to squeeze through. Her beaming face
looked toward the throne as her tiny feet shuffled through the
hall. She weaved in and out of the bowed servants, occasionally
tapping their heads playfully, and nudged her way through the
visitors.

The king's countenance shifted from stern and majestic to warm
and welcoming. Her bare feet sprang up the velvet steps until she
cast herself into the waiting arms of her father. As she whispered,
he nodded, taking in every word. He then rose to his feet and car-
ried her off to tend to her need.

This scene from *Anna and the King* (1999) is a dim reflection of the privilege we have in Christ. The King of glory has made a way for us to call *the* Father *our* Father. Through the Son we are invited to draw near with the assurance that our Father hears: "Let us then with confidence draw near to the throne of grace, that we may receive mercy and find grace to help in a time of need" (Heb. 4:16).

In Christ we are invited to respectfully bound into God's throne room, boldly passing cherubim who cover their faces day and night crying, "Holy, holy, holy" (Isa. 6:3; Rev. 4:8). We are invited to ascend the steps of the Ancient of Days, where outstretched arms receive us without reservation.

Our boldness is not flippant; it's a confident reverence, for we approach the Father's throne clothed in the righteousness of Jesus. Unhindered access to the throne is the privilege of blood-bought children.

Strength from Grace

We need strength to fight sin—just not the kind we usually seek. Shortly after becoming a Christian I was part of a "purity club." Each week we shuffled in and took our seats around a jar of dollar bills. We discussed how our week had gone, either boasting in success or confessing compromise. If we had compromised, we made the walk of shame to lay our penance in the "Pervert Pot." We tried every tactic imaginable to fight sin—willpower, financial fines, excessive exercise, cold showers, increased fiber, and smacking each other after failures—but all to no avail.

The purity to which Jesus calls us cannot be engineered. Shame, self-punishment, and pride are powerless to truly change us for good. The gospel alone has power to transform the human heart (Rom. 1:16–17). While we might affirm this truth in theory, we undermine the gospel we proclaim when we foster a culture based primarily on external performance. Internet filters, accountability groups, and self-imposed boundaries are no match for gospel power. In fact, rules without grace produce self-reliant pride, which callouses the heart. "It is good," then, "for the heart to be strengthened by grace" (Heb. 13:9).

We are continually in need of grace—and Jesus is always ready to supply it. Yet for some reason we forget where strength is derived. A church member once asked his pastor, "Why do you preach the gospel to us week after week?" The pastor replied, "Because week after week you forget it."[1]

Awareness of weakness is a gracious gift, for it keeps our eyes locked on God for help. Have you ever wondered why he allows your sinful struggle to remain? Only the consciously sick know their need for a physician. Only those aware of their poverty sense their need for a generous benefactor. If God were to remove your struggles with lust or anger or anxiety—would he ever hear from you in prayer?[2] Your struggle with sin should cultivate increasingly intimate reliance on God.

Struggle toward Jesus

Freedom from sin is a godly ambition. Growth in holiness really is possible. But we must be patient. Sanctification takes time. There is no microwave maturity in the Christian life; it works like a crockpot. There is no switch to turn off sin's allure; it dies slowly.

God did not fast-track Israel to the Promised Land. He took them on the slow train; one that exposed, corrected, and shaped them. He works in a similar way with us today.

---

1   Some have attributed this story to the German Reformer, Martin Luther.
2   This concept comes from John Owen's *Of the Mortification of Sin in Believers*, in *Overcoming Sin and Temptation*, ed. Kelly Kapic and Justin Taylor (Wheaton, IL: Crossway, 2015), 88.

When we stumble, therefore, we must know what to do. Here the apostle John serves us well: "My little children, I am writing these things to you so that you may not sin. But if anyone does sin, we have an advocate with the Father, Jesus Christ the righteous" (1 John 2:1).

John shares our desire to see evil eradicated, but he is also a realist. When we sin, we must not fall into the ditch of despair or cower in the shadows of shame. Rather, we must look to Jesus.

The word *advocate* means "helper" or "intercessor." It's the same word Jesus uses to describe the Holy Spirit's ministry; it describes one who comes alongside a weaker person to render aid in a time of need.[3] As our risen advocate, Jesus stands to help us when we fall. He is the righteous one who loves to bind wounds incurred during unrighteous wandering (Ps. 147:3).

Yes, we should see and sorrow over sin. Yes, we should mourn the ways we've traded soaring pleasures for selfish lusts. But our spiritual sorrow should not sink us with shame—it should lift our eyes.

When sin strikes, make eye contact with Christ, your merciful high priest:[4]

Since then we have a great high priest who has passed through the heavens, Jesus, the Son of God, let us hold fast our confession. For we do not have a high priest who is unable to sympathize with our weaknesses, but one who in every respect has been

---

3 John 14:16, 26; 15:26; 16:7. According to the *Greek-English Lexicon of the New Testament*, the word in one Central African language would be translated "'the one who falls down beside us,' that is to say, an individual who upon finding a person collapsed along the road, kneels down beside the victim, cares for his needs, and carries him to safety." J. P. Louw and E. A. Nida, *Greek-English Lexicon of the New Testament*, 2nd ed., vol. 1 (New York: United Bible Societies, 1996), 141.

4 See Thomas Watson, *The Doctrine of Repentance* (Edinburgh, UK: Banner of Truth, 1987), 19–22.

tempted as we are, yet without sin. Let us then with confidence draw near to the throne of grace, that we may receive mercy and find grace to help in time of need. (Heb. 4:14–16)

Go to him quickly, continually, and boldly. And don't do it alone.

Go quickly to Jesus. Don't let sin have another moment of glory. Cast it aside and flee to the Lord of love.

Go continually to Jesus. "Draw near" is a standing invitation.[5] You will never wear out your welcome or exhaust his patience. Come; his throne is open to you now.

Go boldly to Jesus. It is not audacious to approach the Almighty when summoned. We'd have no right if we had no Christ, but in him we have the freedom of a child to approach his father's arms. Don't hesitate because you're unworthy. Jesus didn't come to call the righteous, but sinners.

Go together to Jesus. "Let us" draw near, the author of Hebrews says. We are not invited alone. We certainly may come to Jesus by ourselves, but God would also have us come with others. Do not allow shame to hinder the blessing others will receive by helping you to see Christ. They too will see his face and receive mercy.

Too often we are tempted to keep our eyes on our sin and temptation. But if you are always thinking about yourself and your sin and how to avoid it, you will be more likely to fall back into it. Why? Because your heart is set on your sin.

But if your eyes are continually upon Jesus and you think of your sin only in regard to how it can point you to Jesus, you will slowly begin to think less of your sin. Why? Because your heart is set on your Savior.

---

5 The word translated "draw near" is in the present tense, communicating ongoing action.

Sin calls you to look in, but God calls you to look up to Christ. In a letter to a struggling believer, the late Scottish pastor Robert Murray M'Cheyne gave priceless counsel:

> You have been bitten by the great serpent. The poison of sin is through and through your whole heart. . . . Now for the remedy. Look to Christ; for the glorious Son of God so loved lost souls, that he took on him a body and died for us—bore our curse. . . . Do not take up your time so much with studying your own heart as with studying Christ's heart. For one look at yourself, take ten looks at Christ![6]

Looking to Christ helps you see:

1. His righteousness, not your rebellion.
2. His faithfulness, not your failure.
3. His beauty, not your burden.
4. His love, not your lethargy.
5. His glory, not your grief.
6. His mercy, not your misery.
7. His conquest, not your condemnation.
8. His sacrifice, not your sin.
9. His death, averting your destruction.
10. His resurrection, assuring your resurrection.

Our present treasure is that we stand in the righteousness of Christ. Our future hope is that soon we will be taken to a land where sin shall be no more and we will look like Christ.

---

6 Andrew Bonar, *Memoir and Remains of the Rev. Robert Murray M'Cheyne* (Philadelphia: Presbyterian Board of Publication, 1844), 236.

Saved to Sin No More

On that coming day, we will be ushered into a better world. It will be a new land where heaven and earth are united as one.[7] In this place God's purposes will reach their climax, and the church he ransomed with his blood will be saved to sin no more (Acts 20:28).[8]

The apostle John explains: "Beloved, we are God's children now, and what we will be has not yet appeared; but we know that when he appears we shall be like him, because we shall see him as he is. And everyone who thus hopes in him purifies himself as he is pure" (1 John 3:2–3).

Etched on the Almighty's calendar is the great day on which he will send his Son to reclaim his bride (Mark 13:32; Rev. 21:2). His waiting for us, and ours for him, will give way to a glorious union that will cause angels to marvel and every creature to cry, "Worthy is the Lamb!"

The prophet Isaiah gives us a glimpse:

> On this mountain the Lord of hosts will make for all peoples
>> a feast of rich food, a feast of well-aged wine,
>> of rich food full of marrow, of aged wine well refined. . . .
>> He will swallow up death forever;
> and the Lord God will wipe away tears from all faces,
>> and the reproach of his people he will take away from all
>>> the earth,
>> for the Lord has spoken.
> It will be said on that day,

---

7 See Isa. 65:17; 66:22; Acts 3:19–20; Rom. 8:18–25; 2 Pet. 3:13; Rev. 21–22.
8 See William Cowper, "There Is a Fountain Filled with Blood," 1772, hymnary.org/text/there_is_a_fountain_filled_with_blood_dr/.

"Behold, this is our God; we have waited for him, that he
  might save us.
This is the LORD; we have waited for him;
let us be glad and rejoice in his salvation." (Isa. 25:6–9)

Human language is inadequate to capture this world of glory.
Waiting overtaken by wonder. Faith yielding to sight. Futility
eclipsed by beauty. Sorrow swallowed by celebration. Shame slain.
Regret removed. Doubt dispelled. Fear forgotten.

We will enjoy this new world in physical bodies transformed into
glorious ones (1 Cor. 15:35–58). Temptations that once whispered
in your ear will be silenced. Desire will not be abolished; it will
only be met with ever-deepening enjoyment of God.

This, brothers and sisters, is why we sing,

O that day when freed from sinning, I shall see Thy lovely face;
Clothed then in blood washed linen, How I'll sing Thy
  sovereign grace;
Come, my Lord, no longer tarry, Take my ransomed soul away;
Send Thine angels now to carry, Me to realms of endless day.[9]

Holy living in the present is fueled by the holy hope of our future.
In the meantime, let's commit to two things.

1. Cultivate Heavenly Desires

"Where your treasure is," Jesus said, "there your heart will be also"
(Matt. 6:21). Your focus will determine your affections. Be care-

---

9 Robert Robinson, "Come Thou Fount of Every Blessing," 1758, www.hymntime.com/tch
   /htm/c/o/m/e/t/comethou.htm.

ful, then, to "not love the world or the things in the world," for they are "passing away" (1 John 2:15–17). Instead, meditate on Jesus, who awaits you in heaven, and plead with God to help you treasure him above all else.

The book of Revelation promises blessing to those who read and apply its words. This blessing is twofold: we see the glory of Christ, which *warms* our hearts, and we see the folly of sin, which *warns* our hearts.

Fill your mind with the assurance that we will forever be like Jesus. Let your imagination travel to that day. Smell the fruits of the tree of life; taste the banquet where flowing wine brings endless joy. Let the songs of angels and the redeemed drown out the songs of sinful sirens.[10]

Consider how unfulfilling the adulteress's house is when compared to the place Jesus has prepared for us. Be repulsed by the false pleasures that plunge many into eternal destruction, and be wooed by the promised pleasures in the paradise of God. See your name written in the book of life by fingers of mercy. Imagine having a crown set on your head by the one who bore a crown of thorns on his. Envision that moment when you will hear your King say, "Well done, good and faithful servant" (Matt. 25:21).

Such sights will deepen your desire to see him all the more and to indulge sin all the less.

2. Help Others to Heaven

Purity of heart gives us the blessing of seeing God, which compels us to help others see him too. Lust turns our attention inward—

---

10 Isa. 25:6; Matt. 26:29; Rev. 5:9–14.

to soul-shrinking idols that refuse God and use others. Purity of heart, though, compels us outward by keeping Christ's greatness before our eyes. As our love for him increases, so does our commitment to make disciples of all nations.[11]

As we abide in him, our joy is made full, which compels us to help others know his joy too (John 15:1–11). An eternal perspective provokes urgency to call unbelievers to repentance and fuels fervency to help fellow believers persevere.

As we journey toward the Promised Land, facing temptations and trials, we remind each other that "the sufferings of this present time are not worth comparing with the glory that is to be revealed to us" (Rom. 8:18). We embrace the assurance that "this light momentary affliction is preparing for us an eternal weight of glory beyond all comparison" (2 Cor. 4:17).

Marching home, our hearts hum heavenly tunes:

Oh, don't you want to go, to the Gospel feast;
That Promised Land, where all is peace?
Oh, deep river, Lord, I want to cross over.[12]

And soon we shall. That mighty river will be stopped and we will step, together, into the Promised Land (Josh. 3:1–17).[13] There we will unite with the redeemed who have gone before us. We will join their songs of celebration—forever.

11 See Greg Handley's excellent article "How Porn Is Sidelining Missionaries," International Mission Board website, July 19, 2018, www.imb.org/2018/07/19/porn-sidelining -missionaries/.

12 From the spiritual "Deep River," sung by homesick slaves long before it was first printed in *The Story of the Jubilee Singers: With Their Songs* by J. B. T Marsh in 1876.

13 Crossing the Jordan River into the land of Canaan foreshadowed crossing through death into eternal rest with the Lord.

That day may seem distant, my dear struggling saint, but we are now nearer than when we first believed—nearer than when you began this book. Don't lose heart; we're almost Home.

Come, Lord Jesus, come!

Appendix 1

I'm Being Tempted Right Now, Help Me!

YEARS AGO, A MAN WAS hunting deer in the Tehama Wildlife Area of Northern California. As he climbed through a rocky gorge, he lifted his head to look over a ledge and saw something move next to his face. Before he knew it, a rattlesnake struck, just missing him. The strike was so close, however, that the snake's fangs became snagged in the neck of his sweater.

As the snake coiled around the man's neck, he grabbed it just behind its head. A mixture of hissing and rattling filled his ear as he felt warm venom run down his neck. He tried to dislodge the fangs from his sweater but fell backward and slid down the embankment. Using his rifle, he untangled the fangs, freeing the snake to strike repeatedly at his face. The man later explained, "I had to choke him to death. It was the only way out."[1]

---

1   This story, first published in the *Los Angeles Times*, appears in Chuck Swindoll, *The Quest for Character* (Grand Rapids, MI: Zondervan, 1993), 17–18.

When you face temptation, you enter a battle even more dangerous than having a rattler striking at your face. The Scriptures liken Satan to a closely crouching snake or lion who is provoking passions within us that war against our souls.[2] We must choke temptation to death—it is the only way out.

What follows are four ways to fight when temptation strikes.

1. Pray to God

As the dark hour of temptation fell upon Jesus's disciples, he told them twice to "pray that you may not enter into temptation" (Luke 22:40, 46). He knew the pressure they were about to face, and so he reminded them, "The spirit indeed is willing, but the flesh is weak" (Matt. 26:41).

If Jesus told his disciples to pray *before* temptation comes, how much more do we need to pray once it arrives? When temptation calls, you must pray. You need divine intervention to deliver you from the venom of the tempter. You do not need elaborate prayers, just desperate prayers delivered in faith. The Scriptures provide an abundance of examples:

- "Lord, save me" (Matt. 14:30).
- "Lord, help me" (Matt. 15:25).
- "Jesus, Master, have mercy" (Luke 17:13).
- "O Lord, I pray, deliver my soul!" (Ps. 116:4).
- "Out of the depths I cry to you, O Lord! / O Lord, hear my voice!" (Ps. 130:1–2).
- "Lead [me] not into temptation, / but deliver [me] from evil" (Matt. 6:13).

---

2   Gen. 3:1–6; 4:7; 1 Pet. 2:11; 5:8.

- Lord, you promised not to "let [me] be tempted beyond [my] ability," but to "provide the way of escape" (1 Cor. 10:13). Show me the escape!
- "I believe; help my unbelief!" (Mark 9:24).

Prayer lifts our eyes off of sin's disorienting offer and places it on Jesus. Through prayer we "resist the devil" and "draw near to God" (James. 4:7–8). Through it we confess our desire to sin and plead for help to resist it. We ask God to give us strength to choke out the temptation so that sin cannot strike us. When you are tempted, pray to God. He is the one who helps us and will keep us from falling.

2. Flee Right Away

Joseph was handsome, and his master's wife couldn't help but notice. As lust burned in her heart, she offered him an opportunity for a secret affair. But Joseph resisted. He was loyal to his master and, beyond that, said, "How then can I do this great wickedness and sin against God?" Yet her advances continued "day after day" until she finally cornered him alone. She seized him by his garment and said, "Lie with me." Rather than entertain her offer, "he left his garment in her hand and fled and got out of the house" (Gen. 39:6–12).

Joseph ran because he had no other option. He knew he was too weak to resist temptation as long as he was alone with his master's wife. So he choked the temptation—not by staying and fighting, but by fleeing. We must do the same. When temptation corners you, don't flirt with it—flee from it.

Sin wants to convince you that one more click in the search engine or one more minute on the couch or one more round of

inappropriate conversation is manageable. But entertained temptation is like kryptonite to our sinful flesh. The longer we let it linger,
the weaker our resolve becomes.

This is why Paul told Timothy to "flee youthful passions and
pursue righteousness" (2 Tim. 2:22). Do whatever is necessary to
get away from what is tempting you. Close the computer. Delete
the app. Turn off the phone. Run outside. Get in the car and drive.
Do whatever you need to do to flee the voice of temptation.

3. Call a Friend

Emily felt overwhelmed by temptation's onslaught. Being alone in
her house for the weekend offered so many ways to sin. But rather
than fight alone, she called a sister from church. She explained
how weak she felt and asked for help. Her friend told her to pack
a bag and stay with her for the weekend. Emily agreed and, with
her friend's help, avoided Satan's snare.

You cannot fight sin by yourself. God commands us to "exhort
one another every day, as long as it is called 'today,' that none of
you may be hardened by the deceitfulness of sin" (Heb. 3:13). Sin
assures us that asking for help is weak, shameful, and unnecessary.
But this is just one more lie from Satan, who is "a liar and the
father of lies" (John 8:44).

When temptation strikes, reach out to a friend and plead for
help. Do not make excuses. Send a text or email, or make a call
immediately. Tell your friend that you need help. Say something
like, "Would you pray for me? I'm feeling weak toward temptation,
and I need your help."

Sin cannot live in the light. Drag the temptation into the light
of fellowship and enlist others for help. If the person you called
doesn't take you seriously, plead more urgently or call someone

else. Don't give in to discouragement. Keep fighting, but don't fight alone.

4. Develop a Long-Term Plan

When I was young, my father and I often took walks in the woods near our house, which were known to be inhabited by poisonous snakes. During our first walk, he taught me an important lesson: when you come to a fallen tree on the path, step on it, and then step over it. He explained that snakes often rest under trees, so if we stepped right over a tree, we might startle the snake and get bitten. But if we stepped on the tree and *then* over it, we'd create enough distance to evade the strike of most snakes. Today I can't walk along a path in the woods without remembering this lesson.

Avoiding a snake's strike once is good. Developing a pattern to avoid these strikes forever is better. We cannot, of course, keep the tempter from tempting, but we must develop a plan not to go near his den (Prov. 5:8). Over the years, I have developed an intentional plan to "make no provision for the flesh" in order to guard my walk with Jesus (Rom. 13:14).

Jesus exhorted us to "cut off" whatever might lead us to sin against God (Matt. 5:28–30). I have set up numerous barbwire-like protections to make acting out sinful desires difficult. I encourage you to grab a friend and develop a similar strategy. The following questions might help you get started.

- How are you cultivating hope and delight in Jesus?
- What joy-stealing sins are you most prone to give in to?
- If Satan were to tempt you, how might he do it?
- If you were going to access sin, how would you find it?

- How can you dumb down your electronic devices to make sinning in certain ways an impossibility?
- Are there subscriptions you need to cancel? Phone numbers you need to delete?
- Are there accountability subscriptions you should set up?
- When are you most susceptible to temptation? How can you prepare for these times?
- What passages of Scripture have you memorized or marked to quickly access in times of temptation?
- What lies are you most prone to believe, and what passages of Scripture can you fight them with?
- Whom are you regularly confessing your sins to? Whom can you call when you are feeling tempted?

No Regrets

God rarely touches our lives in such a way that we stop loving sin immediately. But as we fight sin and pursue him, he changes our affections. We begin to love what he loves and hate what he hates. Our confidence in willpower fades, and our hope focuses on Jesus, who was tempted and yet resisted in all the ways we have not (Heb. 4:15).

As you begin to fight afresh for joy in God, remember that sin steals your joy. You will never regret resisting sin. You will always regret giving in. Choke temptation by taking refuge in Jesus and the means of grace he provides: pray to God, flee the scene, call a friend, develop a plan.

Appendix 2

Discussion Questions

Chapter 1: Promise

1. What deceitful promises are you tempted to believe that lead you to sin against God? What makes sin's promises so appealing to you?

2. What passages of Scripture have you found helpful to meditate upon in your pursuit of God? How can relying upon God's promises help you war against sin's promises?

3. We defined purity as *an orientation of the faith-filled heart that flees the pleasures of sin and pursues the pleasures of God by the power of the Holy Spirit*. What makes this definition helpful? If you feel it can be improved, how might you redefine it?

4. How have you misunderstood purity in the past? How did it affect your fight against sin?

5. How have you tried to overcome sexual temptation through self-discipline in the past? What has been your experience?

6. How is the idea of looking to God as the power for purity different from what you've heard before?

7. If you were to take inventory on your life, what evidence would there be that God is your great delight? If he is not, what needs to change for him to be so?

Chapter 2: Sight

1. How does sin hinder your ability to behold Jesus?

2. How are you orienting your time, energy, and schedule around intentionally beholding Jesus?

3. Do you mourn your sin against God? Does your sin shock you, or have you grown calloused to its seriousness?

4. Are there sins you engage in while God is watching that you would never do in front of other people? Have you confessed these sins to other believers?

5. What has it been like to grow in beholding Jesus? When is a time you "saw" him most clearly?

6. Would you be willing to lose everything in order to see God more clearly?

Chapter 3: Passion

1. How did this chapter challenge what you've heard from the world about sex?

2. How did this chapter cause you to rethink what you've heard from the church about sex?

3. If you are not married, how did this chapter help you trust God with your sexuality?

4. If you are married, how can this view of sex help you serve your spouse and redefine what "good sex" actually is?

5. How might your view of God and his commands change if you believed that God doesn't just want something from you, but has good things for you?

Chapter 4: Enemies

1. In what ways do you feel the pull of the world toward impurity? How can you intentionally resist it?

2. What sorts of temptations most uniquely entice your flesh? How do you intentionally war against the flesh's cries for satisfaction?

3. How does the discussion of the devil affect your battle for purity? In what ways does Satan war against you?

4. Think about shows, media, and advertisements you've seen recently. What are they offering and what spiritual price tags are they hiding?

Chapter 5: Fallout

1. What leads you to doubt that God could actually forgive and heal you from your sexual sin?

2. How have you experienced God's grace, forgiveness, and healing regarding your sexual sin?

3. Are there any sinful relationships you are currently engaged in that you need to repent of? What scares you about following through? Who can help you find courage to do so?

4. Read what Jesus calls the Great Commandment (Matt. 22:33–40) and then discuss all the ways sexual sin can lead you to violate this command.

Chapter 6: Feed Your Heart

1. How regularly do you engage in the disciplines discussed in this chapter? How might you be helped to take a self-inventory similar to the one Jessie did?

2. Make a list of the things that cultivate your affection for Jesus. Make a list of things that destroy your affection for Jesus. How can you intentionally build into your schedule the things that stir your affections? How can you be intentional to avoid the things that steal your affections?

3. How have you seen your fight against sin affected by engaging or neglecting the disciplines discussed in this chapter?

4. Which of the disciplines do you find most natural for you to cultivate? Which remain most unused for you?

5. What other disciplines have you found helpful to cultivate your love for God and hatred for sin?

Chapter 7: Help Others Home

1. What have you learned about the importance of the local church in your battle for purity?

2. As you've grown in spiritual maturity, how has your view of the local church changed?

3. What hinders you from being willing to help others to follow Jesus? What hinders you from receiving help?

4. If someone were to know you, what would they need to know about your past? About your current struggles? About your future fears?

5. If someone were to help you—hypothetically—what kind of help would benefit you the most?

6. Who currently knows you and helps you? If no one, who are a few people you'd like to approach about filling such a role?

Chapter 8: Enter the Light

1. Do you see your sin as first and foremost against God?

2. Do you usually think first about the personal consequences of your sin rather than your sin being against God? If so, what might this reveal about your heart?

3. What are some passages in Scripture that encourage you to confess sin and assist you in doing so?

4. How do you refresh yourself with the gospel after you've confessed and repented of sin? How can you help others do the same?

Chapter 9: Drop the Facade

1. What tempts you to hold back honest confession of your sin to others? What is the worst that could happen if you came out of hiding? What would be so bad about it? On the other hand, what would be so good about it?

2. Did the Holy Spirit convict you of any unconfessed sins while reading this book? What are they? Are you going to trust God by confessing them or will you choose to stay in the darkness?

3. Whom do you talk to about your sin? Can you give any examples of times you've seen God use honest confession to help you make progress in spiritual maturity?

4. If you don't have someone to confess your sins to, what steps can you make to cultivate these relationships?

5. How can we become the kind of person others will feel open to confess to?

Chapter 10: Sin No More

1. How does Scripture help you know and consider your identity in Christ?

2. Do you believe God can help you to walk in holiness? What tempts you to doubt it?

3. How do you understand the difference between becoming perfect (which we can't) and walking in obedience by the Spirit? Why is understanding this difference essential?

4. What progress have you seen in your pursuit of sexual purity? How have you grown? What evidence of God's grace do you see in your life?

Chapter 11: Slay Your Foe

1. Do you prayerfully ask God to reveal sin in your life?

2. Are there sins you secretly love and do not desire to kill? What makes them precious to you? How does keeping these sins around affect your walk with God?

3. What drastic measures do you need to make against sin that you've been hesitant to take? What makes you hesitant?

4. Are there other reasons you don't slay your sin than the ones given? If so, what are they?

Chapter 12: Embrace the Throne

1. Whom can you talk with about what you've learned from this book?

2. Identify a younger Christian you could ask to read this book with. How could you help him or her grow in the pursuit of Jesus?

3. What is something missing from this book that you think is important?

General Index

Scripture Index